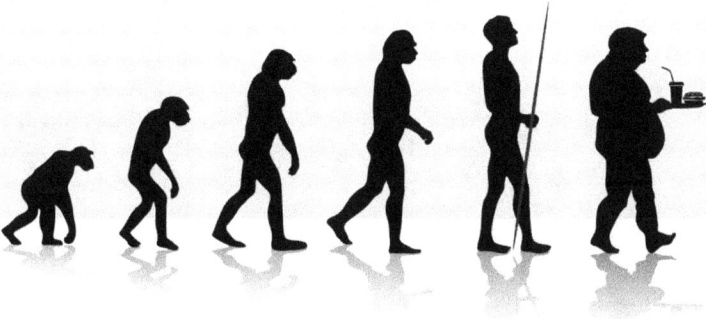

Evolution Evolves:
A Presuppositional Argument Against Naturalism

Evolution Evolves:
A Presuppositional Argument Against Naturalism

T. Dougherty

Sledge Press
Cuyahoga Falls, Ohio

© 2014 Sledge Press

first edition

ISBN-10 0990800806 (paperback)
ISBN-13 978-0-9908008-0-4 (paperback)
ISBN-10 0990800814 (ebook)
ISBN-13 978-0-9908008-1-1 (ebook)

Cover design by David Short, Jr.
Cover image by Ffatserifade, dreamstime.com

www.evolutionevolves.com
www.sledgepress.com

To Anna Wildner,
for putting her copy of Cornelius Van Til's
The Defense of the Faith in my hand some years ago.

Table of Contents

Acknowledgments

A special (and sincere) thanks is due to the American Naturalist philosopher, Daniel Dennett, whose writings, to a great degree, inspired the origination, direction, and title of the present work. I have attempted to take up his challenge:

> I certainly grant the existence of the phenomenon of faith; what I want to see is a reasoned ground for taking faith seriously *as a way of getting to the truth*, and not, say, just as a way people comfort themselves and each other ... (*Darwin's Dangerous Idea*, 154.)

Special thanks is also due to many faithful friends, editors, and accomplices: Sherylyn Dougherty, Ruth Dougherty, Joshua Haveman, Justice Conder, David Short Jr., Reid "Superman" Sharpless, Race MoChridhe, Luke Burke, Jeff Laird (check him out at http://blogos.org/contributors/jlaird/index-jlaird.html), Bonita Jewel, Brittany C. Holmes, Nathan Barnes, Jon Kever, and Jeff Soufal.

The new fundamental feeling: our conclusive transitoriness.
—**Friedrich Nietzsche** *(The Dawn)*

Introduction to Natural Selection

The world around us is full of organized, intricate complexity and appears to have been designed; on this point both Naturalists[1] and Christians agree. Both groups further agree that to have an *actual* design, you would need an *actual* designer. Ultimately, the point of contention is whether this world of complexity has *actually* been designed or whether it merely *appears* to have been designed. Naturalists claim that Charles Darwin's principle of natural selection explains–in the case of organisms anyway–how you can have apparent design without an actual designer. To be fair, the explanation is relatively straight-forward: minuscule genetic variations compounded over very long spans of time among creatures who value the prospect of survival more than the prospect of being eaten by a predator accounts for the present appearance of design in nature. Natural selection explains how you can have "design" without the necessity of a designer, thus rendering the designer superfluous and, according to most Naturalists, counter-productive to true knowledge. In this way, a Naturalist can still speak of "designs" in nature with relative consistency. We see this theme in the influential American philosopher, Daniel Dennett:

---

1   By "Naturalists," I mean those who endorse Naturalism and, by Naturalism, I mean atheistic metaphysical Darwinian Naturalism, the philosophical view that the natural world is all that exists. To simplify things a bit, Naturalism can simply be thought of as atheistic Darwinism.

We know that in the early days–the first few billion years–of life on this planet, self-protective designs emerged, thanks to the slow and non-miraculous process of natural selection. ... Along the way there was much *avoidance* and *prevention*, but at a pace much too slow to appreciate unless we artificially speed it up in imagination. ... Eventually, though, the good designs emerge victorious–or the lineage perishes, which is the much more likely outcome of all these "efforts" at self-preservation of lineage. A few lucky lineages *happened* to "find" good countermoves. (They weren't doing anything, they were just part of what was *happening*–the lucky part, as it happens, that happened to be born with useful mutations). These lucky ones had descendants whose descendants–the lucky ones, again–had descendants, and so forth, till you get to us. We–lucky us–are made of such useful parts, exquisitely designed to be good at contributing to avoidance, but now on a much swifter timescale.[2]

We might say that, with respect to complex organisms, Naturalists believe in *quasi-design*.[3] Dennett, for example, certainly does not believe that organisms have been designed in the sense that, say, Thomas Edison designed the light bulb or Dr. Emmett Brown designed the flux capacitor,[4] for in each of those cases there was a great deal of forethought on the part of some mastermind. Rather, Dennett believes that intelligent creatures fighting for food and survival are very occasionally born with some random genetic variation that just happens to be slightly useful. Those members of the species who happen to be born with this slightly-useful feature naturally have a slight edge over those members lacking this modest upgrade, and if you compound this very slow process over very long spans of time, then you

---

2   Daniel C. Dennett, *Freedom Evolves* (New York: Penguin Books, 2003), 52.
3   The English prefix "quasi" is derived, without much novelty, from the Latin *quasi*, meaning "as if" or "almost."
4   Which is, of course, a fictional time-travel device featured in the *Back to the Future* film series.

can, in fact, imagine "designs" emerging, designs, as it were, in retrospect and hindsight. According to Dennett, "natural selection would inevitably produce *adaptation* … and under the right circumstances, [Darwin] argued, accumulated adaptation would create speciation."[5]

Similarly, if we compare an amoeba and a man from the perspective of Naturalism, seeing the latter as the long-term product of some of the efforts of the former, it is patently true that natural selection tends toward greater complexity and survivability over time. Random mutations appear, and then the fight for survival naturally weeds out the "bad designs" over time. So long as we keep in mind that natural selection has no teleological[6] leanings–no purposes, plans, or goals–it is true that natural selection has made progress. It did not intend to make progress, of course, it is not in any way aimed at making progress, but, from the perspective of man[7] looking back in time in the mind's eye, evolutionary progress is an obvious fact for the Naturalist. Along these lines, Darwin can speak of "new and improved" species arising over time, as the new designs supersede the old designs:

> The extinction of species and of whole groups of species which has played so conspicuous a part in the history of the organic world, almost inevitably follows from the principle of natural selection; for old forms are supplanted by new and improved forms.[8]

Though Naturalists commonly characterize these useful genetic variations as "random," this does not–contrary to many Christian caricatures–actually commit Naturalists to the notion that natural selection

---

5 Daniel C. Dennett, *Darwin's Dangerous Idea* (New York: Touchstone, 1996), 43.
6 Teleology is the theory or study of purpose in nature. Teleology refers to objective purposes, goals, or ends. The question "what is the meaning of life?" is an inherently teleological question, since it supposes that life has some objective purpose or utility.
7 The use of the male pronouns and of "man", "mankind" and such throughout the work are intended to encompass women, of course, as it is certainly not my intention to try to exclude anyone. I simply found this usage to be less distracting within the context of this particular work.
8 Charles Darwin, *The Origin of Species by Means of Natural Selection* (Chicago: Great Books of the Western World, Encyclopedia Britannica, Inc. 1993), 237.

is a random or arbitrary process, for Naturalists believe natural selection is a scientific and mechanical process which operates in accordance with the determinate laws of nature. Just as when Naturalists say "design" they really mean something like "quasi-design," so too when they say "random" they really mean something like "quasi-random." As the evolutionary biologist, Richard Dawkins, explains, "The Darwinian says that variation is random in the sense that it is not directed towards improvement, and that the tendency towards improvement in evolution comes from selection."[9] So it's not that the variations are actually "random" in some literal, substantive sense, and certainly not in any mystical sense, but the point rather is that the process is non-intentional, unguided, not directed toward any particular end. The basic idea is that, sometimes, stuff just happens. Approximately one in 500 humans is born with six fingers on one hand. The extra digit is pretty much always a useless and unwanted freeloader, but it's not particularly difficult to imagine someone–someday–getting one that actually serves some practical function. At a minimum, we can say that there's certainly nothing logically impossible about it. The Naturalist's claim is that mutations emerge in the genetic code, and the only reason the "good designs" happen to stick around over the long term is because they work well in practice and contribute to the survival of those who just happen to be born with them.

> "Naturalism excludes any form of teleology within nature. There is no mind behind nature at all, and certainly therefore, no mastermind."

Thus we discover that Naturalism excludes any form of teleology within nature. There is no mind behind nature at all, and certainly therefore, no mastermind. It is the stuff of myth, from this perspective, to suppose that you were *meant* to be here, or that there is some teleological *reason* for your

---

9   Richard Dawkins, *The Blind Watchmaker* (New York: W.W. Norton & Company, 1996), 438.

being *here* or your *being* in general. Though it may have a nice ring to it, it's not at all true, from this perspective, that "everything happens for a reason." We are the current product (the latest model, you might say) of a very long series of random mutations in a very long struggle for survival, and there is no guarantee whatsoever that our luck will continue to hold out. From the Naturalist's point of view, there is nothing at all *necessary* about the current state of affairs; this is merely how the dice of random genetic variation happened to fall. "If we were to [wind the tape back] and play it again and again, the likelihood is infinitesimal of *Us* being the product of any other run through the evolutionary mill."[10] The only certainty within the framework of Naturalism seems to be *unpredictable evolutionary change.*

We have thus hopefully dispelled one or two common mis-understandings about Naturalism and evaded one or two of the most common strawman arguments that Christian authors sometimes construct. Though it is easy enough to contrast the simple amoeba and the sophisticated human and to caricature the Naturalist as making the gigantic leap between them all in an instant, and then attributing the great deed to the omnipotent power of randomness, this is, in truth, not a particularly fair presentation. To understand a system, you must understand it upon its own terms, and if we Christians are—in a post-Christian culture—to make a compelling case that Christianity is still a viable worldview, worthy of a person's trust and assent, we must make every effort to present our opponents' views fairly, in their clearest and highest expressions.

Naturalism has had a monolithic ascent in the past century-and-a-half and now stands, among worldviews, as an indomitable skyscraper. It has become the orthodoxy of the academic community and the Saturday morning cartoon alike, and there can be no doubt whatsoever that the current result is a rapid and seismic shift in the average person's outlook toward every aspect of life. Even though most folks still cling to some bland and indistinct notion of God—some inoffensive, unobtrusive, all-inclusive, have-it-your-way McDeity—it must be admitted that this really does look a great deal like

---

10 Dennett, *Darwin's Dangerous Idea*, 56.

some sort of opiate of the masses. In most cases, God is invoked simply as an afterthought unto the appearance of persistent meaning, as the proper accessory of the unexamined life. In all such cases, it must be conceded that theism very much resembles the Naturalist portrayal of it–the crutch of those who have not yet come to grips with the notion that their existence has a certain and unambiguous point of termination. As it continues to ascend, Naturalism will inevitably erode away all such rootless spiritual leanings.

The old foundation is slipping away with little resistance and Christian authors have commonly seemed content to mistake symptoms for causes and to let gimmicks stand in the place of argumentation. Every now and again it has seemed as if our overall strategy was to bring down the skyscraper with a marshmallow shooter. From a Christian perspective, the outlook can thus appear bleak on all sides, in light of which, I thought it best to try to approach the subject from a slightly different angle. Given that the marshmallow shooter has not always worked very well from the outside of the skyscraper, my plan is to sneak it inside. What follows is, in essence, a critique of Naturalism upon its own terms, a Naturalistic critique of Naturalism, or, if you like, an evolutionary critique of atheistic evolution, and in those moments where Naturalism seems distracted by the hail of cushy white confections, we will repeatedly examine the Christian alternative.

The Naturalist and the Christian can further agree that everything is at stake in such a debate.

Theism to Naturalism

In broadest outline, our modern era is characterized by the rise of Naturalism and the decline of Christian belief. Like all historical transitions, this one was gradual. Deism and, to a lesser extent, pantheism, intervened between the predominance of Christian theism and the rising tide of Naturalistic atheism. Where Christians have always regarded God as being both absolutely *distinct* from nature, but also intimately *involved* with nature, this conception slowly gave way to those who denied that God is distinct from nature (pantheism) as well as to those who denied he was involved with nature (deism). God was first deemed impersonal, impotent, or indistinct before he was ultimately deemed non-existent. We could say that it has been a steady "descent with modification."[11]

Deists tended to view nature as a mechanism, that is, as a machine upon which order was imposed from the outside. The appropriate analogy was the watchmaker and his watch. Once the watch is fashioned, the watchmaker's involvement is no longer requisite; he merely fades into the background, done with his tinkering and having to tend once again to his own affairs. Contemporary Naturalists, however, reject this conception, for even though it seems to rid us of religious obligation, still it supposes both teleology and metaphysics,[12] inasmuch as machines are always built for

---

11 Darwin uses this phrase commonly in *The Descent of Man* and elsewhere. He would not approve of this quotation in this particular context, of course.
12 Metaphysics is the attempt to characterize existence or reality as a whole. It can be thought of as

some definite purpose within some definite framework. You would still have to recognize the fundamentally teleological character of the universe, inasmuch as watchmakers are seldom found crafting watches without any particular reason for doing so, and you would still need to recognize the watch as relatively insignificant in light of the watchmaker.

Subsequently, over the past century or so, the mechanistic conception of the universe has tended to give way to a more organic conception. Unlike a machine, which is assembled purposely from the outside, an organism has the principle of order inside of itself and seems, at a glance, considered in-and-of itself, self-organizing in a particular sense. From a certain perspective, a seed is both self-designing and self-replicating, and outside help is bound to be counter-productive in most cases. An organism does not need to have order or organization imposed from the outside for it contains these within itself inherently. The material world is viewed as a closed system explainable upon its own terms, and the orderliness and organization we see in nature is explained relatively easily upon the simple assumption that the laws of physics are inherently organized. If organization and information is inherent to matter, in other words, then there is neither need nor justification for positing any sort of divine organizer.[13] The Naturalist's ontology,[14] in a general sense, consists of a chance

> "If organization and information is inherent to matter, in other words, then there is neither need nor justification for positing any sort of divine *organizer*."

---

one's big picture conception of the world. For our purposes, one's "metaphysic" is simply their worldview or philosophy.

13 This would be a natural application of Occam's razor, to opt for the explanation with the fewest assumptions.

14 Ontology can be thought of as a branch of metaphysics concerned with "being" or what exists. From the Greek *ontologia*, "study of being." For our purposes here, I simply mean the Naturalists' explanation or account of what actually exists.

cosmology (e.g., the Big Bang Theory) coupled with some account of abiogenesis[15] (e.g., the Primordial Soup Theory) and the Darwinian principle of natural selection.

Now it will be granted that there is limited consensus among scientists on the first two of these, in which case it seems as though natural selection occupies the important position of under-girding and providing impetus to the system as a whole. Naturalism could fairly be described—and often has been described—as the extension and generalization of Darwin's apparent success in biology to all other disciplines. For even though natural selection only applies to organisms, and so does not explain the *appearance* of design in celestial bodies or ocean tides or even the laws of nature themselves,[16] still, the discovery of biological natural selection gives the Naturalist some occasion for optimism that future scientific endeavors will provide similar compelling explanations for the non-organic world as well. His expectation is that, given enough time, everything will fall into place. After all, the general tendency of Darwinism is to take complex problems and break them down into as many pieces or as many stages as it takes to make them manageable. This is a helpful rule of thumb irrespective of one's personal beliefs about the origin of the world.

Allowing then the gradual historical movement away from the mechanistic conception of the universe under deism toward the inherently-organized organic conception of atheism, many of the principles associated with the older, deistic science

> "We are evolving organisms in an evolving organic world-system, changing creatures in a world of change."

---

15 Abiogenesis is the theory that life can arise from non-living matter, where biogenesis is the theory that life only comes from life.

16 Dennett, for instance, notes that there is "a certain perceived elegance or wonderfulness in the observed laws of physics" presumably indicative of some sort of quasi-design work. (*Darwin's Dangerous Idea*, 180).

still linger but are now fading, as the remnants of an earlier era. It used to be assumed that there were such things as *unchanging, non-evolving, necessary,* and *mechanical* laws of nature, but many men of science are now coming to recognize that this is no longer tenable, for if anything is true about Naturalism it is that things change over time. We are evolving organisms in an evolving organic world-system, changing creatures in a world of change.

Under the old regime, for instance, David Hume (1711-1776), the Scottish philosopher, argued against the possibility of miracles upon the basis of unchanging scientific law:

> A miracle is a violation of the laws of nature; and as a firm and unalterable experience has established these laws, the proof against a miracle, from the very nature of the fact, is as entire as any argument from experience can possibly be imagined. Why is it more than probable, that all men must die; that lead cannot, of itself, remain suspended in the air; that fire consumes wood, and is extinguished by water; unless it be, that these events are found agreeable to the laws of nature, and there is required a violation of these laws, or in other words, a miracle to prevent them? Nothing is esteemed a miracle, if it ever happen in the common course of nature.[17]

And elsewhere:

> A miracle may be accurately defined, *a transgression of a law of nature by a particular volition of the Deity, or by the interposition of some invisible agent.*[18]

---

17 David Hume, *An Enquiry Concerning Human Understanding* (Chicago: Great Books of the Western World, Encyclopedia Britannica, Inc., 1993), (X.I.91).
18 Ibid., (X.I.91).

So then, a "firm and unalterable experience" has epistemologically[19] established inviolable, unchangeable laws of nature, and a miracle is "a transgression" or "violation" of any such law. There simply cannot be miracles because the unchanging laws of nature exclude it. God is bound to act in accordance with my inviolable experience. Today, this argument seems antiquated in some ways, not the least of which is the supposition of *eternal* and *immutable*[20] scientific laws. Hume clearly did not apply his own skepticism consistently enough. Can any amount of induction or experience prove everlasting, unchanging, universally-applicable laws of nature? It's quite obvious that neither my experience nor the sum total of all the experience of the human species can establish inviolable and eternally unchanging laws; not in a Christian world, not in a Naturalistic world, not in any conceivable world. In fact, a recent experiment with respect to the gravitational constant–that classic exemplar of unchanging scientific laws–suggested that gravity is not constant, but changing.[21] Similar suspicions have been raised regarding the speed of light.[22]

Allowing then that no amount of inductive experimentation could prove the *actual* existence of absolute, unchanging, universally-applicable laws of physics or of chemistry or of biology, etc., it follows that such a belief could only be established on

> "if nature changes and evolves, it would take nothing short of a tremendous leap of faith to conclude there were such things as unchanging and non-evolving laws of nature."

---

19 Epistemology is the branch of philosophy concerned with a theory of knowledge. The relevant questions are how do we acquire knowledge, and how can we be sure that the knowledge we've acquired is correct?

20 i.e., unchanging.

21 http://www.newscientist.com/article/dn24180-strength-of-gravity-shifts--and-this-time-its-serious.html#.UzI5iVfLI4Q

22 http://www.livescience.com/29111-speed-of-light-not-constant.html

a deductive basis, assuming it to be so at the outset. While a great many Naturalists still believe in unchanging scientific constants (e.g., gravity, the speed of light constant, conservation of energy, etc.), given that the central theme of Naturalism is unguided, non-necessary, unpredictable evolutionary change, it seems hard to imagine that Naturalism could provide the proper foundation for the deductive assumption that there are such things as unchanging scientific constants. Stated otherwise, if nature changes and evolves, it would take nothing short of a tremendous leap of faith to conclude there were such things as unchanging and non-evolving laws of nature.

After all, if Naturalism depicts nature (i.e., the whole cosmos) as an organism as opposed to a mechanism or machine, it must be added that, where an organism has the principle of order within itself and seemingly contains within itself its own final cause, so to speak–the tomato seed is destined to become a tomato plant, for instance–the same will not hold true of nature from the perspective of Naturalist philosophy. The organism of nature has no final cause, and no guiding principle intrinsic to itself. If it is an organism, it is an organism with no DNA and no destiny. As Dawkins reminds us:

> Natural selection, the blind, unconscious automatic process which Darwin discovered, and which we now know is the explanation for the existence and apparently purposeful form of all life, has no purpose in mind. It has no mind and no mind's eye. It does not plan for the future. It has no vision, no foresight, no sight at all. If it can be said to play the role of watchmaker in nature, it is the blind watchmaker.[23]

Within the framework of Naturalism, what is true of natural selection will be true of nature as a whole. There was (and is) no guaranteed outcome in view as far as the laws of nature are concerned. The current state of things was no more necessary than any other conceivable state, and the future is

---

23 Dawkins, *The Blind Watchmaker*, 9.

certain to be unpredictable. This is just the way things happened to turn out, and any other run through the mill would be vastly different. The laws of science, in their current forms, were no more necessary than any other quasi-random configuration.

An honest Naturalist will concede this point. Obviously, scientific experimentation cannot prove that any particular scientific principle is universally applicable and universally unchanging at all times and in all places. This belief is scientifically unverifiable in principle, and therefore it is, by definition, an empty assumption every time it appears. Obviously, there is nothing logically necessary about the current laws of physics, and there is certainly no guarantee of their eternal security, so to speak, and so an honest Naturalist will concede that physical "laws" are called "laws" only in the loose sense that they are generally applicable with respect to our immediate environment, in the current era, as far as we can tell. To be fair, this isn't really much skin off of the Naturalist's nose. It will not surprise him in the least to discover that he is living in a world of relative truths.

An honest Naturalist will even more readily concede that his "laws" of logic and reasoning are themselves subject to evolution and to unpredictable change. As the product of natural selection, man himself will, in the long run (the very long run, I mean), be supplanted by this or that "new and improved" species, the reasoning of which he could not possibly have anticipated, the thinking of which will undoubtedly be better-adapted to survival, to say nothing about such beliefs being more "true" than our own. As Darwin explained:

> Man may be excused for feeling some pride at having risen, though not through his own exertions, to the very summit of the organic scale; and the fact of his having thus risen instead of having been aboriginally placed there, may give him hope for a still higher destiny in the distant future.[24]

---

24 Charles Darwin, *The Descent of Man and Selection in Relation to Sex* (Chicago: Great Books of the Western World, Encyclopedia Britannica, Inc., 1993), 597.

It is, of course, presumptuous to suppose that whatever species replaces man at the top of the food chain will consider himself human. Such a species would not be *homo sapiens*, by definition. Our "higher destiny" is much more likely to be gawked at from the other side of the glass, as we do with our own animals. Judging by current practice, it appears to be true that the highest animal on the food chain owns all of the others outright, by default. More to the point, since man himself is, of course, subject to this type of macro-evolution,[25] his laws of logic themselves are subject to unpredictable evolution and change, just as the laws of nature are subject to unpredictable evolution and change. It may be objected that our laws of logic are the only laws of logic conceivable, but that's really only to say that they are the only laws of logic conceivable *by us*. Our minds are undoubtedly framed in a particular way, but it must be remembered that there is nothing at all *necessary* about that framing.

> "Our minds are undoubtedly framed in a particular way, but it must be remembered that there is nothing at all *necessary* about that framing."

In his aptly-titled book *Freedom Evolves*, Dennett argues precisely this point regarding free will–our particular set of decision-making faculties came to be at some point, and will be otherwise in the future, assuming that our luck continues to hold out:

---

25 Where micro-evolution is variation within a given species through selective breeding, genetic engineering and so on, macro-evolution is Darwin's idea of speciation arising out of mutation and natural selection. Micro-evolution, in other words, is change within a species, where macro-evolution is the change from one species to another species. Nobody denies the existence of micro-evolution, while some groups (young earth Creationists, for example) deny that macro-evolution ever occurred.

Free will is like the air we breathe, and it is present almost everywhere we want to go, but it is not only not eternal, it evolved, and is still evolving. The atmosphere of our planet evolved over hundreds of millions of years as a product of the activities of simple early life-forms, and it continues to evolve today in response to the activities of the billions of more complex life-forms it made possible. The atmosphere of free will is another sort of environment. It is the enveloping, enabling, life-shaping, *conceptual* atmosphere of intentional action, planning and hoping and promising–and blaming, resenting, punishing, and honoring. We all grow up in this conceptual atmosphere, and we learn to conduct our lives in the terms it provides. It *appears to be* a stable and ahistorical construct, as eternal and unchanging as arithmetic, but it is not. It evolved as a recent product of human interactions, and some of the sorts of human activity it first made possible on this planet may also disrupt its future stability, or even hasten its demise. Our planet's atmosphere is not guaranteed to last forever, and neither is our free will.[26]

Dennett's thesis is perfectly consistent. Our particular set of decision-making faculties arrived on the stage of history only very recently; such faculties are subject to unpredictable evolutionary change, and, given enough time, those faculties will no longer exist. The planet's atmosphere is evolving, and mankind's conceptual atmosphere and thought processes are likewise evolving. We are evolving animals in an evolving world. Our variety of free will is just a blip on the radar of our 12 billion year history.

Yet upon what basis can Dennett conclude that the current laws of mathematics are, as he puts it, "eternal and unchanging?" Do the ideal numbers exist out in space somewhere, eternally independent of mind? Given that Naturalism and philosophical realism (in the Platonic sense, anyway)

---

26   Dennett, *Freedom Evolves,* 10.

are more-or-less polar opposites, it must be conceded that mathematics is an *idea* or, "if you're not into the whole brevity thing,"[27] a *conceptual discipline,* and that conceptual disciplines exist in no shape or form outside of the human mind, and that our mathematics exist, therefore, only as a product and consequence of our evolving minds, and that our mathematics is, therefore, no more eternal than we are, merely another blip. Mathematics is a useful mental fiction conducive unto survival, and that's it. It *appears to be* a stable and ahistorical construct, but it is not.

Similarly, Dennett assures us:

> The law of gravity will never let us down (it will always pull us down, so long as we stay on Earth), and we can rely on the speed of light staying constant in all our endeavors. Some of the stability comes from even more fundamental *meta*physical facts: 2+2 will always add up to 4, the Pythagorean theorem will hold, and if A = B, whatever is true of A is true of B and vice versa.[28]

Free will is a temporary and transient product of evolutionary change, but the "metaphysical fact[!]" of the Pythagorean theorem is everlasting and immutable? Dennett believes that only the physical world exists (that's what Naturalism *is,* after all), so it's not perfectly clear what he means by "*meta*physical facts," but presumably, he just means that the Pythagorean theorem is an *idea,* and that ideas only exist within minds. That being the case, it seems very curious to suppose that metaphysical facts are eternal when the minds containing such facts evolved only very recently and will–with relative certainty–eventually perish. Nature evolves, atmospheres evolve, we evolve, minds evolve, freedom evolves, but the Theorem endures forever? This seems laughably egoistic. When did Dennett become a Platonist? Upon what basis can he assure us that gravity is eternal and unchanging? Has he tested this

---

27 The Big Lebowski, Joel Coen & Ethan Coen, Polygram, 1998.
28 Dennett, *Freedom Evolves,* 9.

in the lab? Has he inferred it from natural selection or from Big Bang? Has he gone back to the future to do a quick double check? It almost seems like Dennett is trying to pull a fast one here. It almost seems like he wants to salvage a few essentials–just one or two eternal, absolute truths–from the fire and from the flux before he allows the rest to be inevitably swept away by the tsunami of certain and unpredictable evolutionary change. Yet here he's simply failing to think carefully about the matter at hand.

One curious fact about nearly every Naturalist is that they seem to assume the principles at work in the process of evolution are themselves not subject to evolution or change. Because precisely therein lies the rub. Though nothing is so fundamental to Naturalism as the fact of unguided, unpredictable, non-necessary, quasi-random change, the Naturalist discreetly tucks a select few timeless absolutes into his back pocket before the start of the hand–the laws of physics, the laws of logic, the system of mathematics, the principle of natural selection, and a host of other things are each, in turn, made immune to the impermanent, unpredictable, and quasi-arbitrary thrust of the system as a whole. Evolution is made curiously immune to itself. The moment it dawns on us, however, that *evolution evolves*, it is as if, in the subjective madness and chaos of the struggle for survival, the system turns finally against itself in order to cannibalize and consume itself.[29] This is all suggestive of the fact that, in actual practice, no system of thought can rid itself of eternal absolutes, while still positioning itself as anything more than the sort of gossip we hear on TMZ. In this light, it seems almost as if all human thought is aimed at capturing and quantifying the unchanging eternal, and cannot be satisfied short of that.

Still, I have to concede that the Naturalist has not lost much. He knows that "on a long enough time line, the survival rate for everyone drops to zero,"[30] and that this is every bit as true of the race and of culture (genes

---

29 Admittedly, this argument (as all of those that follow) would present little problem to a theist who believed that God had governed the development of each successive evolutionary stage. Everlasting absolutes are, of course, consistent with the assumption of an everlasting, absolute God.

30 Fight Club, David Fincher, 20th Century Fox, 1999.

and memes, if you like) as it is of the individual. If Big Bang occurred 12 billion years ago, and our sun will burn out in another 4 billion or so (followed, of course, by the fizzling of every other sun), then it seems to be true that we are, beyond any reasonable doubt, in the sunset of our collective history. The Naturalist will allow that the facts he writes in books are true only in a relative and temporary sense, and he will probably admit that he has at times

> "If Big Bang occurred 12 billion years ago, and our sun will burn out in another 4 billion or so (followed, of course, by the fizzling of every other sun), then it seems to be true that we are, beyond any reasonable doubt, in the sunset of our collective history."

overstated his case, making it sound as if he were talking about eternal Truth which could be depended upon indefinitely into the future. He will concede that his science has all-too-often read more like oracles and revelation.

So let us go yet one step further. We all learned in grade school that the business of science is observation and experimentation in a controlled environment. Now, strictly speaking, it can never be *proven* where the world came from through scientific means, as there exists the possibility of neither observation nor experimentation regarding the original event. Even if we fully granted that all of the requisite mechanisms of Big Bang, primordial soup, and natural selection work perfectly and no gaps or problems remain at all, and even if we could reproduce in a laboratory the explosion of matter (perhaps out of nothing, perhaps not?) and this matter, left to itself, settled into a gentle and affable environment immaculately corresponding to the needs of life, and then some bit of this brainless stuff pulled itself by its bootstraps, as *causa sui*,[31] from non-life to life (why this bias toward life, when inert matter is clearly much better suited to survival than life is?),[32] and then evolved by mutation and selection into some smarter, more-capable, multi-cellular something-or-other, all the way up through the little monkeys who fling

> "On anyone's account, a lot can happen in 12 billion years; of that there can be no doubt."

their poo at one another and the noble great ape, whose eyes–as I have found–are full of wisdom, and we arrived finally at man with his laughter and his moral sensitivity and his weird urge to clothe himself–even if it were possible to reproduce all of this in the lab, still it would not, strictly speaking, prove that the world *actually* came about in this way. For even if it could be proven beyond any reasonable doubt that it could happen that way under the *current* laws of science, when viewed from the perspective of the *current* laws of thinking, this is worlds apart from the belief that the world *actually* arose in this way, under these *particular* laws of physics, when conceived from this *particular* point of view. On anyone's account, a lot can happen in 12 billion years; of that there can be no doubt. As we look back to our past, we shall have to concede that it is something of an imposition to assume that the current laws of human thought and the current laws of nature were in effect when the world came to be. This is merely to read the current system back into some past system that is manifestly unknowable.

And so the conclusion here is modest enough: one's belief about the origin of the world is ultimately, in every last instance, a part of one's metaphysic or worldview or philosophy, which is to say that it is a matter of deductive presuppositions,[33] which is to say that it is a matter of faith in some perceived authority. In the last analysis, it is not the business of inductive science to provide us with a coherent worldview. A coherent worldview is,

---

31 The Latin is, literally, "cause of self."

32 And how does this self-creating first life have the foresight to create itself as a self-replicating thing?

33 A presupposition is something that is assumed in advance. For instance, eyeglasses presuppose eyes, books with words presuppose reading, etc.

in fact, a precondition[34] of science, a subject which we will explore further in the chapter which follows.

---

34 A precondition is simply a condition that must be satisfied beforehand, basically synonymous with "prerequisite."

No Facts Outside of System

Induction is the movement from the particular to the universal, or, in other words, from the individual to the general. If I drop a spoon 100 particular times and each time it tends to fall downward toward the ground upon which I am standing, I might postulate that there is some general principle at work which causes this particular phenomenon of the downward-falling spoon. Perhaps spoons have a natural "attraction" for earths, perhaps the earth is just moving upward and the spoon remained stationary, or perhaps I'm trapped in the Matrix, where machines are using my body as a source of bioelectricity and, objectively considered, "there is no spoon."[35] There are lots of possibilities. At any rate, the point is, based upon particular instances of an observed event, I formulate a hypothesis based on my observation, and then I can test this hypothesis through experimentation in a more controlled environment, trying to remove as much bias and as many variables as possible within my small sphere of control.

Deduction, on the other hand, is moving from the universal to the particular, or, in other words, the general to the individual. "All men are mortal" is the archetypal example. It cannot be proven inductively that all men are, in fact, mortal, for there are many men who have not yet died, and there are more still who have not yet even been born, so many particular test-subjects simply lie outside of the boundaries of possible experimentation.

---

35   The Matrix, Andy Wachowski & Lana Wachowski, Warner Brothers, 1999.

Still, the absence of immortal men in our everyday experience lends weight to our general sneaking suspicion. It is a universal proposition assumed to be applicable to all particular men. If all men are mortal, and I am a man, it follows, of course, that I am mortal in the relevant sense.

As Hume so clearly demonstrated, inductive science fundamentally makes certain deductive assumptions for which no justification can be given upon an inductive basis. Certain things must simply be taken for granted at the outset. To use Hume's infamous example, scientists assume a cause and effect world, in which the effect says something about the cause, but no inductive experiment can prove this proposition. If I were to witness one billiard ball bump into another billiard ball, I assume the motion of the second ball was the effect of the motion in the first ball, that the two incidents bore a causal relation to one another, but, strictly speaking, all I actually saw was the first ball move, and then I saw the second ball move. I didn't actually see the one event "cause" the other event, but merely assumed the two events were connected in a particular way. "Cause" and "effect" aren't the kinds of things that I can experience with my senses, of course. The fact remains that alternate explanations are conceivable as to why the one ball stopped and the other started moving. As Hume explains:

> The mind can never possibly find the effect in the supposed cause, by the most accurate scrutiny and examination. For the effect is totally different from the cause, and consequently can never be discovered in it. Motion in the second billiard-ball is a quite distinct event from motion in the first; nor is there anything in the one to suggest the smallest hint of the other ... [We suppose a] tie or connection between the cause and effect, which binds them together, and renders it impossible that any other effect could result from the operation of that cause. When I see, for instance, a billiard-ball moving in a straight line towards another; even suppose motion in the second ball should by accident be suggested to me, as the result of their

contact or impulse; may I not conceive, that a hundred different events might as well follow from that cause? ...

In a word, then, every effect is a distinct event from its cause. It could not, therefore, be discovered in the cause, and the first invention or conception of it, *a priori*,[36] must be entirely arbitrary. And even after it is suggested, the conjunction of it with the cause must appear equally arbitrary; since there are always many other effects, which, to reason, must seem fully as consistent and natural. In vain, therefore, should we pretend to determine any single event, or infer any cause or effect, without the assistance of observation and experience.[37]

Any experiment designed to prove cause and effect relations would itself undoubtedly have to assume various cause and effect relations, and so it becomes clear that a world of cause and effect must be assumed at the outset of scientific inquiry. It is, in other words, a *necessary assumption* of science. Though it is sometimes supposed that induction and deduction can be neatly isolated, and that induction can be practiced apart from deductive assumptions which are merely presupposed as true in advance, ultimately this view of the matter cannot be defended. You always start somewhere, with a myriad of assumptions which cannot be tested or proven scientifically. There's always one philosophy or another working behind the scenes. As the philosopher of science, Valentine Hepp, explained:

> ## "There's always one philosophy or another working behind the scenes."

The fundamental idea of the inductive method, namely that one can climb from the particular case to the general, presupposes such conceptions as these: the general exists, the

---

36 i.e., assumed deductively prior to experience.
37 Hume, *Enquiry*, (IV.I.25).

particular exists, there is a connection between the general and the particular, and out of all this the genuinely deductive conclusion is reached: therefore, we must be able to reach the general through the particular. Every hypothesis contains a general thesis which we try to perceive out of our experience and experiment. The reasoning which is carried on in that case is deductive in character. It can be formulated thus: if this general thesis is true, then these particulars must agree with it. It is a pure mystification when one pretends that the inductive method ever is applied 'purely.' It is interwoven with the deductive method from beginning to end.[38]

Observation is induction leading to hypotheses which are deductive. In turn, we take the deductive hypothesis and again head back to the field and do some further inductive experiments to seek to "prove" our deductive hypothesis to our satisfaction. Additionally, we were assuming a whole host of things, deductively, before the first observation ever began. In order to conduct the spoon-dropping experiment, I had to assume that I exist, that spoons exist, that my actions can affect a world assumed to be outside of me, that the external world aligns with the principles of my mind, that the external world forms a coherent, rational unity and so forth.

A coherent system of deductive propositions or, in other words, a coherent worldview is therefore the precondition of science. Our inductions must be consistent with our deductive system and our deductive system must provide support for those deductive principles with which we approach our inductive experiments. Our practice, in other words, must be in alignment with our theory, and all practice presupposes or assumes in advance the existence of a theoretical framework of thought. You can never get to practice *except through theory*, in which case it is simply naive to suppose that science itself, considered in isolation, can constitute a coherent worldview.

---

38 Valentine Hepp, *Calvinism and the Philosophy of Nature* (Grand Rapids: William B. Eerdmans Publishing, 1930), 76-77.

Scientists generally assume, for example, that the external world is an ontological unity, such that scientific constants are constant no matter where you go and no matter what era you live in. They assume at the outset that we can "unify" all of the "diverse" facts of experience, such that the cosmos is a "uni-verse," that is, a single coherent whole to which we can apply our deductive hypotheses uni-versally. Where Christianity describes the world as an ontological unity upon the basis that each particular is derived from a single source and is geared toward a particular end, it seems fair to ask, upon what basis can the system of Naturalism assume that the world is, in fact, an ontological unity? Hepp raises an interesting question:

> When you see a sky-scraper in New York, you see it as a unity. The fact that it can be divided into two parts, or that it is made up of many kinds of material, does not alter things. If you meet a man of world-renown, you get the impression of one personality, although his ... body is made up of innumerable small parts. How is that? Because each and every part of the sky-scraper has a purpose given to it by the architect, and it answers to that purpose; because every member of the body has its place and work which it can carry on only in relation to the whole. The same thing holds true for nature ... Everything in nature has a cause, whether material or immaterial, whether known or unknown. Everything has a purpose, the inorganic as well as the organic. For the inorganic world must serve man, in order that man may serve his God.[39]

A thing can only be described as having *unity* upon the basis that it functions as *one unit,* and this seems to be an inherently teleological conception. Whether we think of the cosmos as a mechanism or as an organism or as something else entirely, still it will be true that we are envisioning the whole of nature to be *one thing which performs some function*

---

39   Hepp, *Calvinism and the Philosophy of Nature,* 133-134.

rather than just a big collection of unrelated and discordant things. Within Naturalism, the universe is that unity that "big bangs" every now and again. It is generally supposed that the order resulting from Big Bang was merely incidental, by chance, but such a view clearly cannot support the *necessary assumption* of science that there is a universal and comprehensive order in nature such that the laws of thought and the laws of science can be applied universally.

Scientists assume, in other words, that nature, considered as a whole, is a single orderly system in which all of the parts bear some *real correlated relation* to one another. If "nature" really is *something*, then it has to be *one thing* in some meaningful sense, it must function as a homogeneous unity and it must, therefore, *exist* as a homogeneous unity, as a single machine, but there seems to be no justification at all for this belief within Naturalism. All that exist are particular bits of evolving matter in particular evolving places and particular evolving times and the fact of Naturalistic evolution itself precludes the possibility of a single unchanging unifying principle. It would be much more consistent for the Naturalist to reject the notion of the essential unity of the universe, yet if nature is not a homogeneous unity, that is, a single system or machine, then no justification could be given for the belief that the laws of science and the laws of logic can be applied universally, in the manner of scientific law. In such a world, there would obviously be very little justification for the belief that an experiment conducted in one place would have any bearing upon any other place, or that an experiment carried on at one time would have any bearing upon any other time, in which case it seems clear that Naturalism contradicts applied science to the degree that applied science must assume precisely the opposite.

Let me put it this way. The scientific community routinely assumes that beneath all of the data lies a single coherent framework. It is assumed that the next great theory will encompass several other older theories within itself, providing a higher degree of clarity and opening up new avenues of inquiry and progress. Science is imagined to march in a straight line toward the perfect application of a single theory to all particulars, as if behind the immense diversity of facts in the world lies a single coherent framework, operating at peak efficiency, without any waste. The scientist imagines nature to have a certain streamlined, economical, unified architecture behind it. Yet upon what basis could Naturalism sustain such a belief? With respects to the comprehensive unity of nature, science seems to stand in opposition to the big bang philosophy of Naturalism.[40]

Within the Christian framework, by contrast, fundamental to every fact is the fact that it was created by God, for God's purposes, in God's framework, and so all facts bear an obvious, real, correlated relation to one another. Unity is derived from the fact that God created the cosmos as a unit, that is, as one functional teleological whole with order imposed universally upon it, as a single machine. Nature is the product of one mind, and therein lies its simple unity and coherence. So then, Christianity can, in a mere sentence or two, very easily account for this particular fundamental assumption of science, where Naturalism, when confronted with the marshmallow shooter, seems to buckle clumsily beneath its own weight.

Now, admittedly, it seems as though Christianity has begun to creep in here, unannounced, unproven, and without invitation or justification, as if I snuck it in the side door alongside the marshmallow shooter. By way of framing my argument a bit more clearly, I would simply note two things: first, this work is fundamentally a *Christian apologetic*, and second, it is fundamentally a Christian apologetic *against Naturalism*. I have no intention whatsoever of trying to build a ground-up argument for Christianity, nor will I claim to have *proven* Christianity at any point along the way. The scope of the project and the nature of the argument, rather, is that, as in the prior example, Christianity can very easily explain basic scientific assumptions that Naturalism cannot even begin to explain, and that Christianity is, therefore,

---

40 Though today the Big Bang Theory is generally presented as inherently atheistic, it should be kept in mind that it was originally proposed by a Roman Catholic priest, who believed Big Bang to be compatible with his Christian faith. The Bible says Yahweh spoke creation into existence, and perhaps God's speaking was of an explosive big bang sort; the Bible simply doesn't say. Just as it is necessary to distinguish between a theistic, guided Darwinism and an atheistic, unguided Darwinism, it is also necessary to distinguish between a theistic, guided Big Bang and an atheistic, unguided Big Bang. My arguments are, of course, aimed at the latter, and, admittedly, would be ineffective against the former.

from the perspective of science, a more tenable position than Naturalism is.[41] The vision here is of two foes duking it out in the manner of Rocky Balboa and Apollo Creed.[42] Such an approach must largely ignore other contenders; intermediary positions (such as the general theism of Charles Darwin himself) must be passed over for the simple reason that those arguments would have to take on entirely different contours. Some folks may be annoyed at the contrast of two extremes at the expense of all intermediaries, but, frankly, the movie would have been weird if the Clubber Langs and Ivan Dragos of the world had not been postponed for the sequels. Every person must ultimately assume the truthfulness of their own system; I am a Christian person who accepts the truthfulness of the Christian narrative. My creed will inevitably outpace my argumentation in some instances (it's a short book, after all), a fact for which I can only ask for the reader's forgiveness in advance as I have called attention to it here.

Back to the business of the marshmallow shooter then, science must also assume that its own results are objectively true and trustworthy. Yet, as Alvin Plantinga puts it, "natural selection is interested in adaptive behavior, behavior that conduces to survival and reproduction; it has no interest in our having true beliefs."[43] Within the framework of Naturalism, we are the fortunate products of a chance cosmology, our minds being adapted to survival through a process of random variation and natural selection. As Dawkins explains:

---

41 My argument is largely abductive—inference to the best explanation. Abductive inference is reasoning from a given set of data to a hypothesis that best explains that data. For example, if I leave a full glass of water on the kitchen counter unattended and I return an hour later to find it empty, though an infinite number of explanations is conceivable as to where the water went, only one or two of those explanations is likely to strike me as plausible. I can further narrow the number of plausible options by gathering more information and reviewing the relevant facts of the case. In the context of this work then, we will examine various philosophical and scientific data and then redundantly ask the question whether Christianity or Naturalism better accounts for that data.

42 Naturally, I'm playing the part of the underdog, and, naturally, this is a Rocky II type scenario (given that Rocky lost in the first film).

43 Alvin Plantinga, *Where the Conflict Really Lies: Science, Religion, & Naturalism* (New York: Oxford University Press, 2011), 271.

[We think] objects are "out there," and we think that we "see" them out there. But I suspect that really our percept is an elaborate computer model in the brain, constructed on the basis of information coming from out there, but transformed in the head into a form in which that information can be *used*. Wavelength differences in the light out there become coded as "color" differences in the computer model in the head. Shape and other attributes are encoded in the same kind of way, encoded into a form that is convenient to handle.[44]

That being the case (or anything remotely like it being the case), it's entirely unclear how we can make the leap from this variety of non-necessary adaptive utility to the type of true, universal propositions required by science. The Naturalist must concede that his view of the matter is not "true," strictly speaking, but merely temporarily functional, certain to eventually be outmoded, repealed, or replaced. That being the case, he will not at all begrudge us the liberty of tuning him out in lieu of other, more important matters, such as the new season of *Dancing with the Stars* and our waning MMORPG subscriptions.[45] It is a profound curiosity–a curiosity of curiosities–that even Naturalists don't believe their position is true in a persistent sense. Nietzsche's point here must be granted:

Only if we assume a God who is morally our like can "truth" and the search for truth be at all something meaningful and promising of success. This God left aside, the question is permitted whether being deceived is not one of the conditions of life.[46]

---

44 Dawkins, *The Blind Watchmaker*, 48.
45 MMORPG = massive, multi-player, online role playing (video) game. A lot of the good ones have a monthly subscription fee.
46 Quoted in Plantinga, *Where the Conflict Really Lies*, 314.

Scientists must also presuppose that nature is inherently rational, that nature, considered objectively, as an object, "makes sense." If the rational God made a world that is rational inasmuch as it is a product of his rational mind and he makes man with a rational mind (patterned after his own, in his own likeness and image, a rational copy of the rational original, rational man thinking God's rational thoughts after him), then it seems consistent enough to believe that there's plenty of rationality to go around and that the outside world is rational and intelligible and that we can arrive at universal scientific knowledge. As one of the founders of modern science, Johannes Kepler (1571-1630), stated impeccably:

> Those laws are within the grasp of the human mind. God wanted us to recognize them by creating us after his own image so that we could share in his own thoughts ... and if piety allow us to say so, our understanding is in this respect of the same kind as the divine, at least as far as we are able to grasp something of it in our mortal life.[47]

Upon the principles of Naturalism, on the other hand, it is hard to imagine a possible justification for the belief that nature is rational, and that nature, considered in itself, makes sense, for how could it make sense, when "sense" supposes rationality, and nature, *considered in itself*, bears no relation to any mind? It would be much more consistent within Naturalism to view the "laws of nature" and such as merely the arbitrary imposition of the principles of human reasoning upon the external world. What is true in the case of design will be true in every other case:

> [We seem to have an] intuition that design work is somehow intellectual work. Design work is discernible ... only if we start *imposing reasons* on it ... [What] Darwin provided was the idea that this Intelligence could be broken into bits so tiny and

---

47   Quoted in Plantinga, *Where the Conflict Really Lies*, 277.

stupid that they didn't count as intelligence at all, and then distributed through space and time in a gigantic, connected network of algorithmic process.[48]

Dennett understands that, properly speaking, natural selection never *designed* a single thing and to the extent that we see "designs" here and there, it is obviously true that we are merely imposing our own perspective on the outside world. We come to think that there really are "designs" out there, but, properly speaking, there aren't any designs out there, for "design" is a teleological concept by definition, and nature has no dealings with such things on a Naturalistic account. People design things, but neither natural selection nor nature can "design" anything at all. This is merely us "imposing reason" on that which is inherently non-reasonable, merely us trying to artificially foist teleology and rationality upon a non-teleological and non-rational world. Natural selection may account for the *appearance* of design, but it must always be kept in mind that this appearance is, in fact, a false and profoundly misleading appearance. "Design" is pure illusion, entirely unreal, a mirage that disappears just as you draw near it. It must always be kept in mind that, in addition to being blind, the blind watchmaker doesn't know anything about watches or about watch-making either. In fact, the truth is that the watch itself was an illusion all along; there never was a watch to begin with; the watch was something that we read into it from the beginning.

> "Natural selection may account for the *appearance* of design, but it must always be kept in mind that this appearance is, in fact, a false and profoundly misleading appearance."

---

48 Admittedly, it looks like I butchered this quote, though I do not believe I have. I encourage the reader to go check it out for themself, which brings me, of course, to my footnote: Dennett, *Darwin's Dangerous Idea*, 133, emphasis added.

Naturalists are generally quick to admit that they feel like they're *seeing things* at times–the illusion of design, the apparent purposefulness of life, etc.–but a much simpler explanation is that they *really are* seeing those things. After all, the simplest explanation for the *appearance of design* is bound to be *design itself.* If I see what *appears* to me to be my wife, then the simplest explanation will inevitably be that it *is* my wife, and likewise with design. Apparent design as described by Naturalism is just that–an appearance, a fictitious apparition, a bit of delusion and self-deception.

Along the same lines, we note that science fundamentally assumes that the categories of man's mind align with the natural order, such that the world which I perceive through my senses perfectly corresponds with the reality of the external world. It must be assumed, in other words, that the world constructed in my imagination is a true and trustworthy representation of the world as it actually exists in itself, such that my principles of mathematics and logic can in turn be applied back upon it appropriately and precisely. Again we ask, is it the Christian system or is it the system of Naturalism which best accounts for the perfect alignment of subject and object which science must presuppose? Even Darwin had his doubts:

> But then arises the doubt–can the mind of man, which has, as I fully believe, been developed from a mind as low as that possessed by the lowest animal, be trusted when it draws such grand conclusions? May not these be the result of the connection between cause and effect which strikes us as a necessary one, but probably depends merely on inherited experience?[49]

And elsewhere:

> With me the horrid doubt always arises whether the convictions of man's mind, which has been developed from the mind of the lower animals, are of any value or at all trustworthy. Would

---

49   Charles Darwin, *Autobiography* (New York: W.W. Norton & Company, 1993), 93.

anyone trust in the convictions of a monkey's mind, if there are any convictions in such a mind?[50]

We tend naturally to think of ourselves as *the* species, but Darwin understood that we are more fittingly described as just *some* species. Darwin also had a pretty clear sense of why that bothered him: because it's a death-blow to epistemology. There is nothing at all *necessary* about our mode of thinking, but rather all human language and all human reasoning (including mathematics, logic, science, and everything else) are *non-necessary problem-solving strategies* developed on the fly, as it were, under the weight of evolutionary pressure in an unguided struggle for survival, in which case all human language and all human reasoning are *fundamentally teleological* both in origin and essential character. Nature doesn't have *problems* and it isn't trying to *solve* anything, and it doesn't *design* anything, or have *better* or *worse* designs or make any *progress* whatsoever, and it doesn't contain *mathematical laws* or *algorithms* or concern itself with *validity*, and it doesn't have *species* or *adaptation* or *selection*, and it doesn't contain *physics* or *information-code* and old Mother Nature certainly doesn't know anything about *you* or *me*. If we are her children, we are her forsaken, bastard children.

> "We tend naturally to think of ourselves as *the* species, but Darwin understood that we are more fittingly described as just *some* species."

From this vantage point, it seems obvious that modern science, in its actual practice and application, fundamentally assumes that nature is packed full of *real* intelligence. The scientist assumes that there are real mathematical rules, real designs, and real information-code and such out there in space and in matter. *He assumes that nature has a logical and teleological bent just like the human mind does.* It almost seems as if, even if the scientist verbally denies

---

50   Quoted in Plantinga, *Where the Conflict Really Lies*, 316.

that God created this world, still his practice itself is justifiable only upon the premise that God did, in fact, create this world. He stands, as it were, on borrowed capital, outside the gate plotting sedition.

Let me put it this way from a Christian perspective.[51] Prior to the creation, the omniscient and omnipotent God had a mental projection or a mathematical blueprint in his mind of how he would build it and how it would all function. Because everything went as planned (in the manner of omnipotence), the creation does, in fact, function according to this blueprint; it's all full of intelligence and information and design. Given that the "ideas of the sender and the recipient must be in tune with one another to guarantee certainty of transmission and reception,"[52] it is because the mind of man is a sort of image or copy of the divine mind,[53] a finite representation of the infinite

> "The scientist assumes that there are real mathematical rules, real designs, and real information-code and such out there in space and in matter. *He assumes that nature has a logical and teleological bent just like the human mind does.*"

---

51 Many Christians deny that macro-evolution ever occurred, of course, and it is necessary to point out that, among Christians who accept the macro-evolutionary theory outlined by Darwin, still the process of macro-evolution is regarded as *guided* by the hand of God. Upon this account, God oversees the development of each successive evolutionary link such that the final result is what he intended it to be all along. The important point, as far as we are concerned here, is that, on *either* Christian account, the world as it is at the moment (and at each prior and successive stage) is a necessary world (or at least necessary *enough* to guarantee a true knowledge of God and the success of his revelatory and redemptive work), the world that God created and governs unto his own ends, the world that is, therefore, inherently teleological and inherently rational. Here we see that the Christian view (I mean either Christian view) is in direct contrast to Naturalism, which imagines each evolutionary link to be the result of a non-necessary, unintended, unguided happenstance, and which denies that there is any inherent rationality or teleology in nature.

52 Werner Gitt, *In the Beginning was Information* (Bielefeld: Christliche Literatur, 1997), 60.

53 cf. Genesis chapter 1 (which is printed as an appendix in the back of the book).

mind of God, that man himself can understand and discover and "back in to" the mathematical patterns and blueprints behind things. The Naturalist, at a practical level, acknowledges the existence of the mathematical blueprint and all of the information out there in nature, though he denies the obvious truth that behind every blueprint and behind every piece of information must ultimately stand some mind.

Consider DNA:

A DNA fibre is only about two millionths of a millimeter thick, so that it is barely visible with an electron microscope. The chemical letters A, G, T, and C are located on this information tape, and the amount of information is so immense in the case of human DNA that it would stretch from the North Pole to the equator if it was typed on paper, using standard letter sizes. The DNA is structured in such a way that it can be replicated every time a cell divides in two. Each of the two daughter cells has to have identically the same genetic information after the division and copying process. This replication is so precise, that it can be compared to 280 clerks copying the entire Bible sequentially each one from the previous one, with at most one single letter being transposed erroneously in the entire copying process.

When a DNA string is replicated, the double strand is unwound, and at the same time a complementary strand is constructed on each separate one, so that, eventually, there are two new double strands identical to the original one ... One cell division lasts from 20 to 80 minutes, and during this time the entire molecular library, equivalent to one thousand books, is copied correctly.[54]

---

54 Ibid., 90.

The language of DNA is written in intelligible symbols upon a set medium, likened always to computer coding or words in a book (both of which presuppose volition, purpose, rationality, and design). It is fundamentally a self-replicating coding system—a sort of biological copy machine—and "the coding system used for living beings is optimal from an engineering standpoint."[55] Information is thus buried in all biological material, it functions without any sign of waste, and even the simplest form of life presupposes some such sophisticated copying mechanism. Life, in other words, presupposes both biological copy machines and a terrific glut of biological information to copy. Given that "there is no known natural law through which matter can give rise to information,"[56] it follows, obviously, that information is the stuff of *mind*. Every Naturalist must try his best to forget what every child understands intuitively.

The rise of the contemporary scientific outlook in conjunction with the decline of Christian faith has frequently led to the suspicion that the two were somehow incompatible, as if the compass of objective science points in the opposite direction as the God of the Bible. Yet the influential 20th century philosopher of science, Alfred North Whitehead, who was certainly not a Christian, argued to the contrary, that the proximate source of our belief in a rational and trustworthy nature was the belief in a rational and trustworthy author of nature, namely, the God of the Bible:

> I have [not] yet brought out the greatest contribution of medievalism to the formation of the scientific movement. I mean the inexpungable belief that every detailed occurrence can be correlated with its antecedents in a perfectly definite manner, exemplifying general principles. Without this belief the incredible labors of scientists would be without hope. It is this instinctive conviction, vividly poised before the imagination, which is the motive power of research: - that there is a secret, a

---

55   Ibid., 95.
56   Ibid., 79.

secret which can be unveiled. How has this conviction been so vividly implanted on the European mind?

When we compare this tone of thought in Europe with the attitude of other civilizations when left to themselves, there seems but one source for its origin. It must come from the medieval insistence on the rationality of God, conceived as with the personal energy of Jehovah and with the rationality of a Greek philosopher. Every detail was supervised and ordered: the search into nature could only result in the vindication of the faith in rationality. Remember that I am not talking of the explicit beliefs of a few individuals. What I mean is the impress on the European mind arising from the unquestioned faith of centuries. By this I mean the instinctive tone of thought and not a mere creed of words. ...

I am not arguing that the European trust in the scrutability of nature was logically justified even by its own theology. My only point is to understand how it arose. My explanation is that the faith in the possibility of science, generated antecedently to the development of modern scientific theory, is an unconscious derivative from medieval theology.[57]

Can it be reasonably imagined that the inductive method of modern science would have entered into mankind's consciousness upon the assumption that the world exploded quasi-arbitrarily into being, that consequently life arose quasi-arbitrarily out of some soup, and, subsequently, evolved through random mutations into its current quasi-arbitrary configurations? Naturalism could have never produced a truly scientific method, for science itself stands in opposition to the philosophy of Naturalism. The Naturalist assumes the orderliness and intelligibility of nature, yet he sees the present order as the product of an original unguided explosion! There has even been

---

57 Alfred North Whitehead, *Science and the Modern World* (New York: Free Press, 1967), 12-13.

the assertion that it was an unguided explosion e*x nihilo,*[58] as if those were commonplace and open to observation and experimentation. According to Stephen Hawking, for instance (who, incidentally, seems to believe that his inductions do not require any deductions), "It is not necessary to invoke God to ... set the universe going" because "spontaneous creation is the reason there is something rather than nothing, why the universe exists, why we exist."[59] And because of spontaneous creation "the universe can and will create itself from nothing."[60] According to Hawking, there is no justification for the childish belief that a rational designer created a rational world of real, knowable design and information, for we have instead the obvious, salient, scientific axiom that "spontaneous creation" *created itself* from *nothing*! One can only presume that the corresponding lab experiment involves staring eagerly at nothing for long spans of time.[61]

There are, in short, a whole host of inconsistent and unjustifiable assumptions within Naturalism. To name only the few we have touched on thus far:

- There is the assumption that the non-necessary categories of the non-necessary evolving minds of us non-necessary animals just happen to perfectly align with the likewise non-necessary categories of the external world, such that we can arrive at objectively true and timeless knowledge.
- There is the assumption of universal scientific constants within the framework of total unpredictable evolutionary flux.

---

58   i.e., "out of nothing."
59   Stephen Hawking and Leonard Mlodinow, *The Grand Design* (New York: Bantam Books, 2010), 180.
60   Ibid., 180.
61   And even this would be inconsistent, since the observer himself and the atmosphere of the lab, etc., would be something rather than nothing. In order to avoid cheating, you would have to start with what Francis Schaeffer liked to call "nothing nothing," that is, nothing in an absolute sense, and then you would finally have to subtract yourself from the experiment as well.

- There is the assumption that the system of unguided evolution has been true from the beginning and will remain true indefinitely, and is therefore immune to evolution.
- There is the assumption that nature is inherently rational, while yet bearing no relation to any mind at any point.
- There is the assumption that nature is a homogeneous unity, though without any actual unifying principle.

We have here merely scratched at the surface in a very few pages; from the view inside, it becomes evident that this skyscraper is made of sand and is ripe for trampling.

There has obviously been a great deal of superficiality here. The same man whose theme is the relative arbitrariness of all beliefs and values is, at the same time, still talking of absolute, unchanging, eternal laws of nature, and the total intelligibility of dumb matter. The future will scoff at his schizophrenia. He will need to give up this childishness. Scientific "laws" are merely the vestiges of a forgotten theism, merely the remnant of some long-lost Law-maker. Just as philosophers abandoned the quest for metaphysical, universal, eternal principles to bring supposed facts into systemic unity, so too science will have to follow suit. Science (by which I mean the Darwinian philosophy operating under the pseudonym "science") too must give up its naive modernism.[62] Just as Naturalism signaled the death of philosophy, so too it signaled the death of science, despite the fact that many Naturalists have convinced themselves that their atheistic philosophy is identical to "science." The Naturalist will have to allow that the order and rationality he sees is merely the imposition of his own mind, *a priori*,[63] upon a world that is,

---

62 Speaking very generally, modernism was the cultural temperament of the late 19th and early 20th century in which there was a great deal of optimism that science and technology (and all things modern, such as Darwinism) would cure many of the ills of humanity. The world wars effectively cured that optimism, and hence, post-modernism is the skeptical turn which has since ensued, which tends to view everything as "relative" and, frequently, as absurd.

63 Literally, "from what is before." (It's very tempting just to leave it at that). *A priori* knowledge refers to deductive knowledge that is prior to experience, given that we have a particular set of sensory and cognitive faculties built into us, so to speak, as part of our physiological composition. The issue of *a priori* versus *a posteriori* knowledge may best be understood by contrasting the competing

upon his own assumption, inherently non-rational.[64] He will have to add to this that the categories of his own mind are themselves arbitrary categories, the quasi-random product of an unconscious, unthinking, indifferent happenstance–a blind watchmaker, if you prefer personification. To this he will have to add, furthermore, that he himself is a non-necessary animal, not designed to *know*, not designed for anything, not *designed* at all. As Van Til observed:

> Suppose we think of a man made of water in an infinitely extended and bottomless ocean of water. Desiring to get out of water, he makes a ladder of water. He sets this ladder upon the water and against the water and then attempts to climb out of the water. So hopeless and senseless a picture must be drawn of the natural man's methodology based as it is upon the assumption that time or chance is ultimate. On his assumption his own rationality is a product of chance. On his assumption even the laws of logic which he employs are products of chance. The rationality and purpose that he may be searching for are still bound to be products of chance ...
>
> It will then appear that Christian theism ... is the only position which gives human reason a field for successful operation and a method of true progress in knowledge.[65]

The universe can only be viewed as a unity upon the deductive assumption that it is, in fact, a unity. The world of nature can only be viewed as

---

epistemologies of John Locke and Immanuel Kant. Where Locke viewed man as a "blank slate" and as sensory impressions as making their mark upon us, so to speak, Immanuel Kant largely reversed this order and saw man as imposing his own view on the outside world, given that man approaches the world necessarily from his own perspective, and necessarily with his own set of equipment and faculties.

64 With respect to science, the trouble with the Kantian view is that once subject and object, phenomenal and noumenal, are isolated from one another, all you are ultimately left with is a subject talking about itself. The unifying principle of everything in a Kantian scheme is the individual, and he can never get to the objective world outside of himself. Science becomes mere psychology at that point.

65 Cornelius Van Til, *The Defense of the Faith* (Phillipsburg: Presbyterian and Reformed, 1967), 102.

rational upon the deductive assumption that it is, in fact, rational. The mind/matter problem and the subject/object problem can each only be resolved upon the deductive premise that mind and matter, subject and object *actually do align*, and here it seems that the only view which could reasonably be imaged to bridge such a chasm is that view which posits an Omniscient Unifier, up above all created particulars, guaranteeing the actual alignment of man with his environment as a wise and all-seeing administrator, and then providing man with a clear connection to omniscient interpretation through written revelation, the admission of man into the mind of God.

All of the most basic assumptions of modern science comport much better with the Christian philosophy than the philosophy of Naturalism. Likewise, the proper foundation for science was also its proper and original source. That view which fits the bill logically is the same view which did, as a matter of fact, fit the bill historically. As Hepp reminds us:

> The diagnosis of blindness to the facts of history would have to be made if it were not admitted that especially from the Calvinistic Reformation there issued forth a power which cleared the atmosphere in favor of a good development of the natural sciences. It certainly is not coincidence that the brightest stars in the heaven of natural sciences rose just in those countries where Calvinism was dominant.[66]

The American physicist and philosopher of science, Thomas Kuhn, in his influential book *The Structure of Scientific Revolutions,* noted the structural similarity between Protestant theology and modern science.[67] Inductive science starts by examining the data and then proceeds to theory and hypothesis. It then proceeds to experimentation in which the theories themselves must submit again to the data, to be observable and repeatable. The inductive data–the facts of nature–are designed to occupy the central

---

66 Hepp, *Calvinism and the Philosophy of Nature,* 35.
67 See, for example, the first paragraph in chapter 11. Thomas S. Kuhn, *The Structure of Scientific Revolutions* (Chicago: University of Chicago Press, 1996), 136.

position of authority. Nature itself is, from beginning to end, the sole point of reference. The task of the scientist is to take nature as it comes to him, upon its own terms, not trying to impose his own views upon it. He must exegete the book of nature by trying to remove personal bias. He must not merely rely on Aristotle or on scholastic or ecumenical authority, but must go to the book of nature itself, to take up and read, as it were, and he must be held to his own findings, recognizing that, within the scientific community, it is neither right nor safe to go against the data, given that any view which ignores the data is bound to defeat itself in the long run. The methods of modern science are designed to ensure that we have done exegesis (reading out of) rather than eisegesis (reading into) the book of nature. The man of science must, in short, trust and obey the text of nature. He must subject himself unto its authority, to stand in its light, to learn its language and to grasp its symbols and types. As Galileo:

> [Natural] Philosophy is written in that great book which ever lies before our eyes–I mean the universe–but we cannot understand it if we do not first learn the language and grasp the symbols in which it is written. This book is written in the mathematical language, and the symbols are triangles, circles and other geometrical figures, without whose help it is impossible to comprehend a single word of it.[68]

Modern science is thus, in a manner that is really quite straight-forward, begotten of Protestant biblical interpretation, the application and generalization of a submissive textual exegesis to the book of nature.[69]

And that being the case, we find ourselves now in the odd predicament that the very wellspring and foundation of modern science–the Christian

---

68 Galileo Galilei (1564-1642), The Assayer (1623), quoted in E. A. Burtt, *The Metaphysical Foundations of Modern Science* (Atlantic Highlands, 1992), 75.

69 I am certainly not saying that Protestantism was the *sole* source of modern science. The emphasis on mathematics, for instance, owed much more to Greek sources than to Hebrew sources. The point is simply that Protestantism played an obvious role in the development of the scientific method.

religion–is seemingly renounced by its own offspring! Here again is that age-old anti-wisdom in which the creature denies its creator and proves itself unworthy both of its own heritage and of the promised inheritance.[70] Science progresses now despite itself, impelled by the waning inertia imparted from a former age, and clearly the "modern science" of old is fading fast, a specter on the death bed, a mere shadow of its former glory.

---

70   cf. Romans chapter 1.

Interpretation and Hammering

"Truth" is, in the ancient turn of phrase, "that which is." We can define truth, loosely, as propositional description, the content of which corresponds to reality. If there are such things as zombies, it would be true to say "there are such things as zombies," whereas if there are no such things as zombies, it would be false to say "there are such things as zombies." A true statement accurately depicts or symbolizes reality, where a false statement does not accurately depict or symbolize reality.

We can easily generalize this principle and say a true worldview or thought-system is that system of propositions which expresses the truth about the world, when taken as a whole. If the world came about through an uncaused Big Bang, then the system of Naturalism is the true system. If, on the other hand, the uncaused Triune Yahweh (i.e., the God of the Bible) created the world, then the Christian system is the true system.[71] There are, of course, other competitors out there as well.

---

71 Among Naturalists there is a common straw-man argument (hardly even worthy of a footnote) that if God is used to explain the current order, then we need something to explain God. As Dennett, "If God created and designed all these wonderful things, who created God? Supergod? And who created Supergod? Superdupergod? Or did God create himself?"(Darwin's Dangerous Idea, 71). This argument is pure hypocrisy for Naturalism also asserts the original eternal unexplained self-existence of some organized prime mover, namely, matter, energy, the immutable laws of physics, mathematics, the Theorem, unguided big bang, etc. To Dennett I ask, who created big bang? Super big bang? And that? Superduper big bang? (This is the "it's my ball and I'm taking it home now!" of arguments, and, by the way, it's your serve). Any explanation of the origin of the world is going to assume some prime mover or be content with skepticism and regress.

We can reasonably infer from this definition of "truth" that true propositions naturally tend to produce better results than false propositions when put into practice. If there are zombies outside, and I tell you there are *not* zombies outside, it would naturally work out much worse for you than if I had told you the truth, namely, that there were zombies out there. Or, if you like, take a more serious example. The heliocentric theory tells us that the earth revolves around the sun, and now-a-days we all believe that this system (a sort of sub-system, I suppose, of a coherent worldview) best accommodates all of the facts and makes for more accurate predictions of future astronomical events within our solar system. In short, the heliocentric theory works, and it works because it is true.

Now this very elementary account of truth and falsehood is complicated by the fact that sometimes a false proposition or system of false propositions can account for some of the facts some of the time, and it is also true that there can be positive developments in science and technology resulting even from a faulty theory. To continue with the example of the heliocentric system, from the time of Aristotle up until the Age of Reason, when Western man believed, more-or-less universally, that the sun orbited the earth, he got very adept at making the facts fit into his faulty framework. Astronomers were able to accurately predict lunar and solar eclipses and a whole host of other astronomical phenomena despite the fact that their underlying interpretive system was completely faulty. The astronomer somehow made it all work, which is to say he *forced* it all to work. Ultimately, of course, the geocentric system tended to stunt real development. It had become complicated and unruly as a result of trying to cram all of the facts into a faulty model. As Kuhn put it, "the state of [geocentric] astronomy was a scandal before Copernicus' announcement."[72] Copernicus' heliocentric theory had the advantage of being mathematically much simpler. The primary evidence in favor of the heliocentric theory was not that it better aligned with human experience (for misnomers like "sunset" and "sunrise" still point to the fact that it's subjectively obvious to us that the sun moves and that we do not

---

72   Kuhn, *The Structure of Scientific Revolutions*, 67.

move!), but rather that it reduced the needed number of assumed epicycles (i.e., planetary orbits) from more than 80 to only 34.[73] It could, in other words, do the same work in less than half the time. The Copernican system better aligned with the reality of the external world, which naturally meant the facts fit into the framework with much less resistance. In other words, all of the pieces of the puzzle fit into place with far less twisting, cutting, or hammering involved.

Having said then that there can be no induction without deduction, no objectivity without subjectivity, no facts outside of a worldview or philosophy, it follows that science is not merely robotic fact-gathering, but rather *human interpretation*. The examination of any fact presupposes a system, and each fact is always interpreted in light of the system. All reasoning, in other words, is circular reasoning, not in the sense that all reasoning involves a logical fallacy, but in the sense that all people think in terms of their own system and interpret their reality in light of that system. Each of us assumes (and cannot but assume) that we are more-or-less correct in our views and that everyone who thinks otherwise is, more-or-less, an idiot, and there is obviously a very high degree of circularity to this. The system itself determines the type of evidence you go looking for in the first place. The system itself gives you a *default set of assumptions and expectations* as to what you are likely to find out there. The system itself

> "Each of us assumes (and cannot but assume) that we are more-or-less correct in our views and that everyone who thinks otherwise is, more-or-less, an idiot, and there is obviously a very high degree of circularity to this."

---

73 Nancy R. Pearcey & Charles B. Thaxton, *The Soul of Science: Christian Faith and Natural Philosophy* (Wheaton: Crossway Books, 1994), 65.

determines the method with which you approach the data and the criteria under which the inductive data is presumed to have proven the deductive hypothesis. Data that doesn't fit neatly is bound to be hammered into place or ignored. As Kuhn explains:

> Closely examined, whether historically or in the contemporary laboratory, [the scientific] enterprise seems an attempt to force nature into the preformed and relatively inflexible box that the paradigm supplies. No part of the aim of normal science is to call forth new sorts of phenomena; indeed those that will not fit the box are often not seen at all. Nor do scientists normally aim to invent new theories, and they are often intolerant of those invented by others. Instead, normal-scientific research is directed to the articulation of those phenomena and theories that the paradigm already supplies.[74]

Before a piece of scientific equipment can be built to measure some phenomenon, a theory is needed to tell the scientist how to build it. The theory tells him what he is looking for, what he should discover, and the theory provides the criteria under which the measurement-experiment will be considered a success. As Kuhn explains, the process is more circular than open-ended:

> Science does not deal in all possible laboratory manipulations. Instead, it selects those relevant to the juxtaposition of a paradigm with the immediate experience that that paradigm has partially determined. As a result, scientists with different paradigms engage in different concrete laboratory manipulations.[75]

---

74 Kuhn, *The Structure of Scientific Revolutions*, 24.
75 Ibid., 126.

The same rule is applicable to worldviews in general. All people interpret every aspect of their world from the vantage point of some particular over-arching system, and all of the individual facts are always interpreted in light of the system. Both Naturalism and Christianity are systems of that sort–comprehensive interpretive grids or filters through which every fact must inevitably pass. Those facts which don't fit neatly through the filter will either be forced to fit or simply ignored.

An analogy might be helpful. Take any book that is subject to dramatically divergent interpretations. In Western culture, the Bible is undoubtedly the most obvious example. When I read the Bible, since I am a particular person, who lives in a particular culture, with particular beliefs and values, I come to it with a host of biases. Right or wrong,[76] I come to it with the assumptions that it is a true book, written by human agents who were inspired of God. It goes without saying that an atheist would obviously read the Bible much differently than I would. His reading, just like mine, would be profoundly shaped by his default assumptions going into it. The atheist comes to the text assuming that it is a collection of diverse mythologies, awkwardly cobbled together into one large disjointed book, and that, therefore, there must be inconsistencies and, lo and behold, he finds inconsistencies. I come to the text assuming it is true, inspired of the Holy Spirit and preserved over time by the Holy Spirit, and that it must therefore be consistent and, lo and behold, I find consistency. My assumption about it has me reconciling things, just as his assumption has him searching for incompatibilities, and both of us discover precisely what we went looking for in the first place. The data itself was identical for both of us, of course, but our default assumptions led us in completely opposite directions in terms of both our method and our corresponding conclusions. The atheist will accuse me of imposing an artificial unity on the text just as surely as I will accuse him of imposing an artificial disunity on the text. Our starting assumptions completely determined the nature of our conclusions. Our inductive "experiments" were completely determined by our respective deductive systems. Our "science"

---

76   For the rightness or wrongness of it is not the point here.

was completely determined by our philosophy. Really, the most profound way of putting it is garbage in, garbage out. As we glare in the general direction of one another, both the atheist and I would agree on this point.

Let's sharpen up the focus here just one more degree. It's also true that when I come to the Bible, I already have in mind a preconceived notion of what I think it says and what I think the Christian system *is*. Now, believing as I do that I need to obey God's teachings (given that I am a sort of submissive Calvinistic Protestant),

> "An unbiased self would be no self at all, a self without values, beliefs, commitments, or dispositions."

when I read it, I hope to spot points of disagreement between my idea of what the Christian system is and the actual system as found in the Bible, and thereby to make some progress in my understanding of it. I consciously try to submit to the data, in other words. Sometimes, however, I have to admit that I like my own system so well, and consider my own system so inerrantly clever, that I gloss over this or that passage or beat this or that text into submission. I take things out of context, I over-complicate things, I ignore distasteful facts, and so forth and so on in order to make the pieces all comport with one another inside a single system, to form a single coherent metaphysical picture. I harden my heart to the voice of the Spirit of God speaking through the word of God.[77] Now at this point, obviously, we will have a great deal of difficulty trying to imagine a "pure" exegete or interpreter without any biases or preconceived notions. An unbiased self would be no *self* at all, a self without values, beliefs, commitments, or dispositions.

We see then that the notion of pure induction or of "hard data" is a myth by any standard. As Dennett put it, "there is no such thing as a philosophy-free science: there is only science whose philosophical baggage is taken on

---

77 Every now and again though—by the grace of God—I make some progress and I reject my system in light of the Bible's system, and I amend my thinking. In my own estimate, I am doing well when my system is losing ground, for, as it is written, the least will be the greatest. (cf. Luke 9:48)

board without examination."[78] As Kuhn put it, "there is no such thing as research in the absence of any paradigm."[79] Among the tools that he brings to the field, the scientist brings his worldview. Wherever he goes, he always tends to bring his own outlook along with him. The deeper his commitment to his system (regardless of what motivates his belief and regardless of whether he is even aware that he has a system), the more he is willing to beat the facts into submission and to hammer them into their proper place. At some level then, it seems obvious that each of us believes what we *want* to believe. We are the free market consumers in the supermarket of ideas. Such is the weight and such is the glory of our existence.

Now despite all this talk of circularity and self-referentiality, we need not resort immediately to the outer darkness of utter skepticism, for if we may liken worldviews to languages, the simple fact is that they're all translatable into one another. They all have some measure of overlap simply given that we live in a particular world in which our minds are framed in a particular way.[80] The human mind has an impressive (ostensibly infinite) capacity to temporarily adopt any number of differing points-of-view, and the prior three chapters all presuppose that meaningful discourse can take place across systems, that a Naturalist and a Christian could, at least in principle, partake in meaningful conversation, and if the reader grant me *any* measure of success at all, seemingly this point must be granted. My project so far has been to take facts formally agreed upon by two systems (primarily, to this point, some of the basic assumptions of applied science), and to see which system is better suited to accommodate those facts. By and large, Darwinian Naturalists and Christians agree, of course, that we live in a real, objective world with real, objective facts and that any sustainable, viable worldview must give a consistent and coherent account of every last one of those facts. That's no simple task, of course. Many a fine system has succumbed to the bludgeoning of the tide of history and has been lost forever, the main reason being that a faulty framework is bound to show some awkward seams here

---

78 Dennett, *Darwin's Dangerous Idea*, 21.
79 Kuhn, *The Structure of Scientific Revolutions*, 79.
80 The Christian way of saying it, of course, is that man is made in the *Imago Dei*, the image of God.

and there and to reflect some dents here and there indicating that some hammering has occurred.[81] Such seams and dents become more obvious over time as they are exploited by the system's opponents, and any system that fails to give a coherent account of any one of the facts of nature or of culture or of anything else is bound, in the long run, to get *left behind* like Kirk Cameron.[82]

Take the following as a clear example of hammering on the part of the Naturalist. In the context of Darwin's *Origin*, the principal argument for macro-evolution (i.e., speciation through natural selection[83]) is what biologists call "homology." The Darwinian belief that homology (anatomical similarity) proves Darwinian evolution is nicely summarized by the zoologist Mark Ridley:

> The ear-bones of mammals are an example of a homology. They are homologous with some of the jaw-bones of reptiles. The ear-bones of mammals did not have to be formed with the same bones as form the jaw of reptiles; but in fact they are [the same] … The fact that species share homologies is an argument for evolution, for if they had been created separately there would be no reason why they should show homologous similarities.[84]

Now the incontestable fact-of-the matter (i.e., the formally agreed-upon fact between the Naturalist and the Christian) is that, as we peruse all

---

81 It's also probably true that none of us operates exclusively out of a single system. Theologically speaking, the import of the apostle Paul in chapter 1 of the letter to the Romans is that the natural man has at least two basic systems. He is both a knower and a suppressor.

82 Just substitute "Nicholas Cage" for "Kirk Cameron" if you're reading this post-2014.

83 Again, micro-evolution (change within a species) must not be confused with macro-evolution (change from one species to another). Many Christians deny macro-evolution, of course, but nobody denies micro-evolution. We can and do see examples of micro-evolution everywhere. For example, the tomatoes I buy at Walmart taste like plastic wiffle balls because they're cross-bred more for durability than taste, since they have to be able to endure the long trip up from Mexico. Tomatoes (as all other organisms) are adaptable within certain limits. That's very different, of course, from believing that tomatoes can evolve into some other, completely different organism over a long span of time.

84 Mark Ridley, *The Problems of Evolution* (Oxford: Oxford University Press, 1993), quoted in Dennett, *Darwin's Dangerous Idea*, 136.

of the animal species within nature, we see stark similarities across various species, as in Mr. Ridley's example above. Admittedly, macro-evolutionary theory can and does explain these puzzling similarities quite simply and quite well–they look similar because they have a shared evolutionary history, a shared lineage and descent at various points in the past. That point being entirely granted, if we tarry here another moment to contemplate the fact that every creature under the sun is flesh and blood and DNA, membrane over muscles and organs, dependent on food and water, having faculties corresponding to these basic needs, for both the intake and the dispelling of them, then we see that, in the first place, the argument from homology probably proves far too much. Every last creature under the sun shares a very high degree of anatomical similarity with every other creature under the sun. Given any two creatures, there will literally be thousands of similarities between them, in light of which, a fossil record with a lot of similarity is simply a given. A great number of the world's systems can and do give a coherent account of homology, and, for that matter, it's hard to imagine *anyone*–ancient or modern–denying that all creatures have certain similarities one with another. Generally speaking, creatures beget offspring that are like themselves, they protect their young, they eat food, they get fat if they eat too much, they have arms and legs and faces, etc. There's nothing particularly modern about such beliefs, of course; it's not as if prior to the publication of Darwin's *Origin* in 1859 it was universally denied that all creatures have certain anatomical similarities. It may very well be true that in all of the world's history, nobody *ever* denied it. In isolation, the fact of homology therefore proves *precisely* absolutely nothing, for the data only speaks when it is interpreted in the light of some philosophy.

If, from this point, we tarry a moment longer to consider that every creature under the sun is a sort of mirrored image of vertical symmetry–one symmetrical nose and one symmetrical mouth, with one symmetrical eye and one symmetrical ear on each side of nose and mouth, as a sort of unfolding reflection of itself, as the opening of a book from the middle, and that there is here a profound degree of beauty, style, and grace, then we see homology pointing clearly in the opposite direction of Naturalism. Why is it that an infinite series of non-necessary random mutations each adds up to architectural symmetry, not just here and there, but seemingly down to the very last creature?[85] Why is it that every last one of these quasi-non-designs looks like an exquisite Greek sculpture, beautiful from an aesthetic standpoint and optimal from an engineering standpoint? Naturalism may explain functionality and it may explain similarity, but only bare functionality and only bare similarity. The *design, artistry,* and *purpose* in nature don't fit into the box, and so they aren't seen at all. As the Naturalist proceeds to "beat nature into line,"[86] his own system becomes a sort of punishment to him. Even when Naturalists do see design, artistry, or purpose in nature, they must quickly convince themselves that they're merely *seeing things* which aren't really there. They are, at some level, aware of their self-deception.

> "Even when Naturalists do see design, artistry, or purpose in nature, they must quickly convince themselves that they're merely seeing things which aren't really there."

Going back to square one then, anatomical similarity, strictly speaking, does not by any means even *suggest,* let alone *prove* an evolutionary link between two species, for any number of alternate explanations could account for the same genetic similarity—such as that one in which a single Designer got it right the first time. All Vincent van Gogh paintings share certain similarities, of course, as having originated from a certain Vincent van Gogh, and, in the same way, the assumption of a single *designer* would account for anatomical similarity across species, even if it were further

---

85 And it's not merely one infinite series of non-necessary random mutations, but practically an infinite number of infinite series of random mutations that each adds up to architectural symmetry!

86 (Kuhn would most likely not approve of this quotation. That seems to be a bad habit of mine for which I am presumably unrepentant). Kuhn, *The Structure of Scientific Revolutions,* 135.

assumed that Darwinian macro-evolution never occurred and was simply a popular modern myth. A Naturalist might respond that such a view would not be very scientific, but that would beg the question of course, and be entirely circular, since he has defined what "science" is in the light of his own system, deductively, beforehand. He is committed to his atheistic definition of "science," and, being somewhat blind to this fact, he strikes down any competing definition, because any competing definition appears absurd to him from the perspective of his own self-referential system. If we're going to live in a relativistic, pluralistic culture, then we really must get much better at it.

We see then that the one looking for God in homology finds God, while the one looking for an atheistic universe in homology finds an atheistic universe, and that the facts of the case align infinitely better with the former. Where comprehensive biological symmetry is inexplicable on a Naturalistic account, for Christians of every sort this is a matter of simple and uncomplicated expectation. An unguided Big Bang and an unguided process of macro-evolution require an endless trail of waste and useless baggage, but in the real world, we discover neither. Strictly speaking, there is no hard data supporting the Darwinian theory of macro-evolution, for there is no hard data, period. There are simply no facts outside of a system or apart from a presupposed metaphysic or philosophy. Here is a nice quote for potential detractors: the so-called "common sense" must be rejected. There can be such a thing as a Naturalistic science, or a Christian science, or a deistic science, or an Islamic science, or a Hindu science, or a Zoroastrian science, and so on, but the notion of a science-in-general, or, in other words, a philosophically-neutral science is a persistent and untenable myth of Enlightenment culture.[87] In a pluralistic culture, a plurality of sciences is inevitable,[88] though we can rest assured that, over time, wisdom will be vindicated by her children.

---

87 Dennett says he is willing to entertain rational arguments regarding God as a possible "extra category of belief worthy of special consideration" (Darwin's Dangerous Idea, 154), but here he has clearly failed to recognize his own bias. If God exists, God is not an "extra category" but rather the fundamental principle of all reality, the fundamental category by which to measure all other categories, the category apart from which no other category can be understood properly at all.

88 In the United States, there is a profound and growing injustice in this regard. Naturalism, because

As we have said, Naturalism is the belief that the natural world is all that exists. Among the most basic beliefs of the Naturalist, therefore, is the notion that God does not exist. The Naturalist sets off on his journey in search of a godless universe. Even though God is the simplest explanation for design, rationality, ontological unity, biological symmetry, teleology, etc., that possibility will be automatically over-ruled in every instance. Given that he set out upon the premise that God does not exist, the only way a Naturalist could ever come to the conclusion that God *does* exist is by being inconsistent with himself at some point along the way.

> "Like the laws of logic, science is an empty set of general principles and best-practices that proves nothing by itself, and depends entirely upon which premises are first brought to the table."

His only hope, in other words, is to be lousy at what he does. Thus we see very clearly that Naturalism is fundamentally a philosophy, and equating it with science is, frankly, an insult to science. Like the laws of logic, science is an empty set of general principles and best-practices that proves nothing by itself, and depends entirely upon which premises are first brought to the table.

---

it does not identify itself as a religious system, appears to pass the test of separation of church and state and automatically receives the nod of approval from state educational systems, where state educational systems frequently get sued if they allow the teaching of theism or more overtly religious systems. Constitutional government cannot endorse a religious system, of course, but neither should it automatically endorse an atheistic system! The whole point, it seems to me, is that the government should not and cannot be in the business of endorsing systems. With respect to public education, the *Land of the Free* has curiously become the Land of the Free-to-teach-atheism-only.

Pre-War Teleology

No evolutionary critique of evolution would be anywhere near complete without a stop along the way devoted to ethics. In conformity with our overall program, here we will attempt to look at ethics from the perspective of Naturalistic Darwinism, as inside the skyscraper rather than outside. Historically considered, Naturalism has produced two very different attitudes toward ethics–the current pervasive moral relativism was preceded by the eugenics movement. While this chapter is dedicated to an exposition of the ethic of eugenics, the chapter which follows is dedicated to the contemporary historicism.[89] All but the most obtuse of readers will understand that I am not *actually* a eugenicist and that, therefore, none of the views presented in this chapter are actually my own. To understand a system, however, you must understand it upon its own terms, and I will, to a certain extent, adopt a sort of apologetic voice unto that end.

The eugenics movement can be described quite easily in broad outline. Natural selection, as we have seen, favors good designs over bad designs and inexorably weeds out bad designs over time. To many Naturalists, this seemed to suggest that man too should strive to promote good designs and to exterminate bad designs in conformity with natural selection.

---

89 By "historicism," I mean the idea that all moral codes are relative to the context of their particular culture and that moral codes cannot be deduced or inferred from general, universal, absolute principles (such as divine commandments).

From a contemporary perspective, two objections present themselves immediately. First, from the outset, Darwinism was historically significant because it didn't require a teleological drive or teleological explanation for the appearance of design in nature. Indeed, Darwinism renounced teleology in nature and served, therefore, as a logical precursor to today's systematic atheism. That being the case, it appears to be a faulty imposition of teleology to try to help natural selection along as if natural selection was out to accomplish something. Second, even if we counter-factually[90] supposed that natural selection *were* trying to accomplish something, how would we have any way of knowing what that was? It should be fairly plain at this point that Naturalistic evolution is unpredictable in principle, and it betrays a certain level of arrogance to think that we are in a position to interpret the ways and means or the comings and goings of natural selection. Thus, contemporary Naturalists unequivocally and seemingly universally renounce the eugenics movement as an inconsistent practical application of Darwinian principles, and, in the name of full disclosure, this is important to point out from the outset.

Allowing then that no contemporary Naturalist actually adheres to the eugenics ethic, an exposition of a position that no one *actually* holds is bound to look like little more than a bit of mud-slinging in this particular context. Still, it should be fairly plain by now that there aren't any guarantees concerning a happy future in a Naturalist framework, and, in fact, the eugenics movement still shows plenty of signs of life. Dawkins, for instance, has recently suggested opening a new dialogue on the subject of positive eugenics:

> "Darwinism renounced teleology in nature and served, therefore, as a logical precursor to today's systematic atheism."

---

90   i.e., contrary to the facts.

In the 1920s and 1930s, scientists from both the political left and right would not have found the idea of designer babies particularly dangerous–though of course they would not have used that phrase. Today, I suspect that the idea is too dangerous for comfortable discussion ... and my conjecture is that Adolf Hitler is responsible for the change. Nobody wants to be caught agreeing with that monster, even in a single particular. The specter of Hitler has led some scientists to stray from "ought" to "is" and deny that breeding for human qualities is even possible. But if you can breed cattle for milk yield, horses for running speed, and dogs for herding skill, why on Earth should it be impossible to breed humans for mathematical, musical or athletic ability? Objections such as "these are not one-dimensional abilities" apply equally to cows, horses and dogs and never stopped anybody in practice.

I wonder whether, some 60 years after Hitler's death, we might at least venture to *ask* what the moral difference is between breeding for musical ability and forcing a child to take music lessons. Or why it is acceptable to train fast runners and high jumpers but not to breed them. I can think of some answers, and they are good ones, which would probably end up persuading me. But hasn't the time come when we should stop being frightened even to put the question?[91]

Let's start here: before Darwin published *Origin* in 1859, there was a prevalent notion in the West that all men were *created equal.* Darwinian Naturalism seemed to challenge this notion on two fronts. First, in a Naturalist scheme man is obviously not *created*, and, beyond that, allowing that bad designs die out and good designs march on, natural selection also seemed

91   Richard Dawkins, *Afterword* in *What is Your Dangerous Idea?*, Edited by John Brockman (New York: Harper Perennial, 2007), 299-300.

to suggest that there is a certain level of *inequality* among the members of any given species. Individuals are thus neither created nor equal, and are obviously not, therefore, created equal. Around the turn of the century, for instance, the Austrian physician, Max Nordau, argued that inequality within any given species is both an obvious fact and an important driver of evolution:

> We, who stand on the ground of the scientific world view, recognize in the inequality of living things the impetus for all evolution and perfection. For what is the struggle for existence, this source of the beautiful variability and the many forms of nature, other than a constant confirmation of inequality? A better equipped organism makes its superiority felt by other members of its species, diminishes their portion at the meal provided by nature, and stunts their possibility for the full development of their individuality, in order to win more space for its own [progeny] ... the least perfect individuals will be destroyed in the struggle for first place and will disappear ...[92]

Beginning with the 5th edition of *Origin*, Darwin began using the phrase "the survival of the fittest" (coined by Herbert Spencer in 1864, after reading *Origin*). To many, this suggested an important teleological motive behind natural selection along with a clear affirmation of inequality among individuals. In light of natural selection, the *survival* of the species is of the utmost importance, and some are simply *more fit* for the job than others.

About two decades after the publication of *Origin*, Robby Kossman, a German zoologist and medical professor, concluded that the relative value of any given individual is to be measured upon the basis of their relative fitness:

> The Darwinian world view must look upon the present sentimental conception of the value of the life of a human individual as an overestimate completely hindering the progress

---

92   Quoted in Richard Weikart, *From Darwin to Hitler* (New York: Palgrave Macmillan, 2004), 92.

of humanity. The human state also, like every animal community of individuals, must reach an even higher level of perfection, if the possibility exists in it, through the destruction of the less well-endowed individual, for the more excellently endowed to win space for the expansion of its progeny ... The state only has an interest in preserving the more excellent life at the expense of the less excellent.[93]

The idea is simple enough. Destroying the least fit leaves more room and more food for the more fit. At some level, it cannot really be denied that the weak and the sick cost us time and money and may very well inhibit the ability of the strong individual to flourish in the struggle for survival. In 1922, Darwin's son, Major Leonard Darwin, argued precisely that:

Political authorities should take into account the enormous burden that degenerates impose on the nation. The sums spent on legislation, criminal justice, and the police exceed £48 million per year. And that is not the whole charge ... If the community had to pay less for degenerates of all kinds, healthy men would have less to pay ... Every rise in taxation is a step towards the degeneration of the race.[94]

Along similar lines, Darwin's cousin, Francis Galton, coined the term eugenics (from the Greek *eu* and *genes* meaning "well-born") in 1888.[95] To give a more precise definition, eugenics is the science of promoting favorable hereditary traits within a species through promoting the reproduction of those members with such desirable traits (positive eugenics), and through discouraging the reproduction of individuals lacking the desirable traits (negative eugenics). It is the science of promoting good designs and weeding

---

93 Quoted in Weikart, *From Darwin to Hitler*, 2.
94 Quoted in Andre Pichot, *The Pure Society: From Darwin to Hitler* (Brooklyn: Verso, 2001), 207.
95 Steven Kuhl, *The Nazi Connection* (New York: Oxford University Press, 1994), 4.

out bad designs, in other words. The general theme was clearly expressed by the jurist Hans von Hentig in 1914:

> The idea, though today it disgusts us, that one could breed humans, like we have bred other animals for the sake of certain useful characteristics, will become important, familiar, and fruitful.[96]

Man is, definitionally within Darwinian Naturalism, an *animal*, a more sophisticated replication of some "lesser" animal, different in complexity, but not different in *kind*. While man behaves objectively with respect to his livestock (i.e., the "other animals," as von Hentig put it), with respect to himself and his own mate, he is full of confused unscientific subjectivity. He talks of "soul-mates" and "true love" and all sorts of subjective nonsense. Darwin taught us that man is an animal among animals, and he should try to look at himself objectively, as from the outside, as an animal. Ideas such as the "sanctity" of human life (note the religious undertone) and the marital "covenant" instantly evaporated. Many eugenicists promptly began promoting polygamy and "free love," as it is (unfortunately) called, and, according to the contemporary historian Richard Weikart, "even the eugenicists who remained committed to monogamy generally exalted eugenics considerations above traditional sexual mores. In their view, sexual morality–like all morality–was only valid inasmuch as it was useful to advance the evolutionary process."[97]

> "man is an animal among animals, and he should try to look at himself objectively, as from the outside, as an animal."

---

96   Quoted in Weikart, *From Darwin to Hitler*, 79.
97   Weikart, *From Darwin to Hitler*, 144.

The eugenics movement flourished not just in Germany, but throughout most of the western world prior to the world wars. In the United States, Madison Grant, president of the New York Zoological Society, wrote in 1916:

> Mistaken regard for what are believed to be divine laws and a sentimental belief in the sanctity of human life tend to prevent both the elimination of defective infants and the sterilization of such adults as are themselves of no value to the community. The laws of nature require the obliteration of the unfit, and human life is valuable when it is of use to the community or race.[98]

Likewise, the French social Darwinist, Clement Royer, in her 1862 preface to her French translation of *Origin* argued that the protection of the weak and sick tends only to make the race as a whole *weaker* and *sicker*:

> What is the result of this exclusive and unintelligent protection accorded to the weak, the infirm, the incurable, the wicked, to all those who are ill-favored by nature? It is that the ills which have afflicted them tend to be perpetuated and multiplied indefinitely; that evil is increased instead of diminishing, and tends to grow at the expense of good.[99]

The weak and the sick tend, of course, to produce offspring who are weak and sick and thereby inhibit the relative health of the race. From the perspective of the survival of the race as a whole, supporting the weak and the sick seems something like poor hereditary hygiene. No shrewd farmer would try to breed defective livestock, or to allow defective livestock to steal food from the healthy and strong, but that is precisely what we do when we promote social programs designed to help the weak and the sick. Helping

---

98   Quoted in Weikart, *From Darwin to Hitler*, 10.
99   Quoted in Weikart, *From Darwin to Hitler*, 89.

the sick and weak is entirely counter-productive unto the end of natural selection which tends, of course, to get rid of the sick and the weak. If there is a cancer in your arm it is better to cut off the arm than to let it corrupt the entire body. Around 1909, the physician and German parliament member, Eduard David, wrote:

> This process of natural selection is frustrated through institutions of social assistance, which aim at preserving the life of damaged organisms, allowing them to reproduce and also preserving the lives of their progeny with inferior health.[100]

The contemporary response indicated above–that we can't tell who the weak links are–falters entirely when talking about the weak and the sick who are weak links, more or less, by definition. Weikart's remarks are conservative:

> All the early leaders [of eugenics] considered eugenics a straightforward application of Darwinian principles to ethics and society. Darwin's cousin, Francis Galton, the founder of modern eugenics, developed his ideas upon reading Darwin's Origin of Species ... Alfred Ploetz, who founded both the German Society for Race Hygiene (the first eugenics organization in the world) and also one of the first journals devoted to eugenics ... informed a friend in 1892 that his main ideas about eugenics were drawn from Darwinism ...[101]

Eugenicists were also quick to point out that the purifying work of natural selection is carried on against the backdrop of war and death. According to Darwin, the struggle for existence is a scientific "law, leading to the advancement of all organic beings, namely, multiply, vary, let the strongest live and the weakest die."[102] And elsewhere:

---

100 Quoted in Weikart, *From Darwin to Hitler*, 83.
101 Weikart, *From Darwin to Hitler*, 15.
102 Quoted in Weikart, *From Darwin to Hitler*, 73.

Thus, from the war of nature, from famine and death, the most exalted object which we are capable of conceiving, namely, the production of the higher animals, directly follows.[103]

War and death are, in Darwin's view, important drivers of evolutionary progress. War and death provide the context in which natural selection does its important, purifying work, the most important work "which we are capable of conceiving."[104] In 1909, Max von Gruber, professor of hygiene (i.e., eugenics) at the University of Munich, said that war and death are indispensable elements of community health:

> The never-ceasing struggle is, according to [Darwin], not useless. It constantly clears away the malformed, the weak, and the inferior among the generations and thus secures the future for the fit. Thus only through the inexorable extermination of the negative variants does it provide living space for the strong and its strong offspring, and it keeps the species healthy, strong, and able to live.[105]

The German zoologist, Heinrich Ernst Ziegler, said that:

> According to Darwin's theory wars have always been of the greatest importance for the general progress of the human species, in that the physically weaker, the less intelligent, the morally lower or morally degenerate peoples must give place to the stronger and the better developed.[106]

---

103 Darwin, *Origin*, 243.
104 Note that Darwin's emphasis here is teleological. The notion of "importance" presupposes teleology—important for what? Important unto what end?
105 Quoted in Weikart, *From Darwin to Hitler*, 74.
106 Quoted in Weikart, *From Darwin to Hitler*, 171.

The Darwinist publisher, Theodor Fritsch, around 1914, argued that we must vehemently oppose all forms of social assistance for the weak and the sick:

> We do not approve of any false humanity. Whoever seeks to preserve the degenerate and depraved limits space for the healthy and strong, suppresses the life of the whole community, multiplies the sorrows and burdens of existence, and helps rob happiness and sunshine from life. Where human power cannot triumph over sorrow, there we honor death as a friend and redeemer.[107]

In a world where natural selection does all the heavy lifting with respect to weeding out bad designs, it was routinely argued that man has the moral obligation to pitch in and to help out. According to the German physician, Wilhelm Schallmayer, "the right of the stronger, that asserts itself in the victory of the better adapted forms over the less perfect, reigns not only in nature, but also in human social history."[108] According to the German anthropologist, Felix von Luschan, the right of the stronger supersedes any rights assumed by "the sick, the weak, the dumb, the stupid, the alcoholic, the bum, the criminal," for all of these "are inferior compared

> "In a world where natural selection does all the heavy lifting with respect to weeding out bad designs, it was routinely argued that man has the moral obligation to pitch in and to help out."

---

107 Quoted in Weikart, *From Darwin to Hitler*, 55.
108 Quoted in Weikart, *From Darwin to Hitler*, 35.

with the healthy, the strong, the intelligent, the clever, the sober, the pure."[109] Ernst Haeckel, the most prominent Darwinist at the turn of the century, argued that for the physically and mentally handicapped, "a small dose of morphine or cyanide would not only free this pitiable creature itself, but also its relatives from the burden of a long, worthless and painful existence."[110] According to Weikart:

> Only in the late nineteenth and especially the early twentieth century did significant debate erupt over issues relating to the sanctity of human life, especially infanticide, euthanasia, abortion, and suicide. It was no mere coincidence that these contentious issues emerged at the same time that Darwinism was gaining in influence. Darwinism played an important role in this debate, for it altered many people's conception of the importance and value of human life, as well as the significance of death.[111]

And elsewhere:

> Those skeptical about the role Darwinism played in the rise of advocacy for involuntary euthanasia, infanticide, and abortion should consider several points. First, before the rise of Darwinism, there was no debate on these issues, as there was almost universal agreement in Europe that human life is *sacred* and that all innocent human lives should be protected. Second, the earliest advocates of involuntary euthanasia, infanticide, and abortion in Germany were devoted to a Darwinian worldview. Third, Haeckel, the most famous Darwinist in Germany, promoted these ideas in some of his best-selling books, so these ideas reached a wide audience, especially among those

---

109 Quoted in Weikart, *From Darwin to Hitler*, 95.
110 Quoted in Weikart, *From Darwin to Hitler*, 147.
111 Weikart, *From Darwin to Hitler*, 75.

receptive to Darwinism. Finally, Haeckel and other Darwinists and eugenicists grounded their views on death and killing on their naturalistic interpretation of Darwinism.[112]

All morality was defined unto the preservation of the best of the human species, unto the end of promoting human evolution. The strong individual, it was argued, has the right to cast off the burden of having to carry along the weight of the inferior, and, likewise, the strong nation has both the right and the duty of unburdening the race of weaker and inferior peoples whose existence serves only to dilute both the food supply and the genetic integrity of the race as a whole.[113] According to the German anatomist Herman Klaatsch, "The humanitarian nonsense which grants equal rights to all on the premise of the unity of humanity, is to be condemned from the scientific standpoint."[114] As we have said, there are differing levels of adaptation among any given species, and this applies to the human species just as surely as it applies to all of the other species of brutes. According to the German publisher and pundit, Theodor Fritsch, "Knowledge about the distinctions between the human species and races belongs to the most recent results of scientific research. We have to admit that the slogan of the equality of all who bear a human face cannot withstand a rigorous examination."[115]

> "there are differing levels of adaptation among any given species, and this applies to the human species just as surely as it applies to all of the other species of brutes."

---

112 Ibid., 161, emphasis added.
113 Our contemporary conception of genes and genetics effectively replaced the earlier idea of heredity. The important point, however, is that, regardless of what era you live in, it's obvious that our children *carry us onward* in certain senses.
114 Quoted in Weikart, *From Darwin to Hitler*, 116.
115 Quoted in Weikart, *From Darwin to Hitler*, 123.

The Darwinian ethnologist Friedrich von Hellwald, in 1875, defined the movement in a nutshell, by arguing that the struggle for existence is "the motive principle of evolution and perfection, in that the weak are worn down and must give place to the strong; so in world history the extermination of weaker nations by the stronger is a postulate of progress."[116]

The prime candidate for extermination was, in most cases, the black man. The German ethnologist, Oschar Peschel, editor of the leading German journal on geography and ethnology, argued that there was physiological evidence for the racial inferiority of the black man:

> The Negro is far removed from the European and close to the ape through its small build, through the relatively small breadth of its skull, through its relatively long upper limbs, and further the relatively short length of the thigh ... Also the Negro is more animal, in that it gives off a disgusting odor, distorts its face in grimaces, and its voice has a harsh, grating tone.[117]

Haeckel, in *The Natural History of Creation* (1868), argued that:

> between the most highly developed animal soul and the least developed human soul there exists only a small quantitative, but no qualitative difference, and that this difference is much less, than the difference between the lowest and the highest human souls, or as the difference between the highest and lowest animal souls.[118]

There is, in Haeckel's view, "much less" difference between the ape and African than between the African and the Caucasian. Haeckel ranked 10 human "species," most fit to least fit, most evolved to least evolved, with Europeans at the top of the list and black-skinned Africans and Tasmanians

---

116 Quoted in Weikart, *From Darwin to Hitler*, 81.
117 Quoted in Weikart, *From Darwin to Hitler*, 112.
118 Quoted in Weikart, *From Darwin to Hitler*, 90.

(i.e., indigenous Tasmanians and aboriginal Australians) at the bottom. In his view, Africans and Tasmanians were the closest human descendants of the gorilla. Unlike the contemporary Naturalist who needs an endless series of "missing links" to fill up the infinite chasm between monkey and man, Haeckel didn't need this in his system, for black people already filled this missing-link role. There were even apparently attempts to artificially inseminate Africans with ape sperm and vice versa.[119] According to Haeckel, not everyone is created equal, but rather, "a single well-educated German Warrior, though unfortunately they are now falling in droves, has a higher intellectual and moral value of life than hundreds of the raw primitive peoples ..."[120] According to the German physiologist, Ludwig Büchner, the African's physiological traits prove his close ancestral connection with the monkey:

> Man is thus essentially distinguished at first glance from his cousins the anthropoid apes by his prominent forehead, broad and strongly developed. In this respect, however, the Negro serves as a transition between man and animal, his forehead being narrow and receding, which coincided with a weak development of the anterior cerebral lobes; also in the Negro, the general conformation of the brain and whole structure of the body offer numerous simian analogies ... the Negro brain is ... inferior in type, imperfectly developed; it is reminiscent on the one hand of the brain of the European neonate, and on the other of that of those animals most closely related to man.[121]

Haekel and Büchner were not novel in their views, for they merely borrowed the main outline from Darwin himself. Given a long process of macro-evolution, we would naturally expect to find a long series of gradations, and many intermediate species between monkey and man. In the real world, however, we do not see such a series of gradations nor do we

---

119 Weikart, *From Darwin to Hitler*, 110.
120 Quoted in Weikart, *From Darwin to Hitler*, 187.
121 Quoted in Pichot, *The Pure Society*, 258.

see the evolutionary hodgepodge that we would more naturally expect to see, but rather we see very distinct, very discreet "species" of creatures (neatly categorized as "reptiles," "mammals," etc.), and we see a tremendous chasm between man and all other creatures. Darwin's answer was that all of the intermediary steps must have died out, and, furthermore, inferior forms will continue to die out:

> At some future period, not very distant as measured by centuries, the civilized races of man will almost certainly exterminate, and replace, the savage races throughout the world. At the same time the ... ape ... will no doubt be exterminated. The break between man and his nearest allies will then be wider ... instead of as now between the negro or Australian and the gorilla.[122]

According to the contemporary French historian, Andre Pichot:

> Far from Darwinism having had the anti-racist effect that legend attributes to it, it actually gave biological support to racism (which it certainly did not invent), as well as a biological foundation for the hierarchical ranking of races ...[123]

Weikart is characteristically conservative:

> To be sure, Darwinism does not necessarily imply scientific racism, and scientific racism did not necessarily depend on Darwinism, but the two shared affinities that made them not only compatible, but also alluring to each other. Historically Darwinism and biological racism are linked tightly together, as many historians have demonstrated. In the late nineteenth

---

122 Darwin's *Descent of Man*, quoted in Pichot, *The Pure Society*, 259.
123 Pichot, *The Pure Society*, 261.

and early twentieth centuries, we almost always find them in tandem.[124]

Natural selection, from the human perspective, presupposes good designs and bad designs. Some have an edge in the struggle for survival. Natural selection, therefore, presupposes inequality among the ranks of any given species. It is therefore true by definition that not all humans are created equal, and it seems, therefore, very plausible that some "races" of man are better equipped than others with respect to survival. Even if it does suppose a certain level of arrogance to assume that we could decipher who was the fittest, a eugenicist would argue that even if our best guesses were wrong, still it would be true by definition that the fittest will always come out on top. Whoever is left standing at the end is the fittest, just as simple as that. According to the German anthropologist, Otto Ammon:

> In its complete effect war is a good deed for humanity, since it offers the only means to measure the powers of nations and to grant the victory to the fittest. War is the highest and most majestic form of the struggle for existence and cannot be dispensed with, and thus also cannot be abolished.[125]

The German artist and journalist Rudolf Cronau was sent to the United States as a correspondent for a newspaper back home. He wrote that one could see the process of natural selection at work in the destruction of the natives:

> The current inequality of the races is an indubitable fact. Under equally favorable climatic and land conditions the higher race always displaces the low, i.e., contact with the culture of the higher race is a fatal poison for the lower race and kills them.

---

124 Weikart, *From Darwin to Hitler*, 116.
125 Ibid., 197.

... [American Indians] naturally succumb in the struggle, its race vanishes and civilization strides across their corpses. ... therein lies once again the great doctrine, that the evolution of humanity and of the individual nations progresses, not through moral principles, but rather by dint of the right of the stronger.[126]

According to the German ethnographer, Friedrich Ratzel, the extermination of Native Americans was a case in point:

And can we any longer doubt the existence of natural selection, when we read, how the last remnant of primitive people melt like snow in sunshine, as soon as they come into contact with the European, and how the European peoples for three centuries have populated entire large continents.[127]

According to Oscar Schmidt, professor of zoology at the University of Strassburg:

If we contemplate the ethnology and anthropology of savages, not from the standpoint of philanthropists and missionaries, but as cool and sober naturalists, destruction in the struggle for existence as a consequence of their retardation (itself regulated by the universal conditions of development), is the natural course of things.[128]

We must learn to look at things not as missionaries but as cool and sober Naturalists. Nature destroys the weak to make room for the strong; it renders bad designs obsolete by way of war and death, period. Old Mother Nature doesn't know anything about kindness, forgiveness, compassion, or self-sacrifice. As one sympathetic politician put it:

---

126 Quoted in Weikart, *From Darwin to Hitler*, 183.
127 Quoted in Weikart, *From Darwin to Hitler*, 193.
128 Quoted in Weikart, *From Darwin to Hitler*, 190.

A stronger race will supplant the weaker, since the drive for life in its final form will decimate every ridiculous fetter of the so-called humaneness of individuals, in order to make place for the humaneness of nature, which destroys the weak to make place for the strong.[129]

The *value* of a life must be measured upon the basis of one's relative fitness:

> While nature only allows the few most healthy and resistant out of a large number of living organisms to survive in the struggle for life, people restrict the number of births and then try to keep alive what has been born, without consideration of its real value and its inner merit. Humaneness is therefore only the slave of weakness and thereby in truth the most cruel destroyer of human existence.[130]

Though we have limited information about the actual sources of Hitler's thought, it is obviously true that Hitler's rhetoric frequently bears a striking similarity to that of Darwin and the leading proponent of Darwinism in Germany, Haeckel. For example, according to Darwin, Haeckel, and Hitler, "The gulf between the lowest creature which can still be styled man and our highest races is greater than that between the lowest type of man and the highest ape."[131] According to Weikart, "Darwinian terminology and rhetoric pervaded Hitler's writings and speeches, and no one to my knowledge has ever even questioned the common assertion by scholars that Hitler was a social Darwinist. It is too obvious to deny."[132] Elsewhere, Weikart notes that:

---

129 Hitler's *Mein Kampf,* quoted in Weikart, *From Darwin to Hitler,* 211.
130 Hitler's *"1928 unpublished manuscript,"* quoted in Weikart, *From Darwin to Hitler,* 215.
131 Hitler's *"1933 statement,"* quoted in Weikart, *From Darwin to Hitler,* 216.
132 Weikart, *From Darwin to Hiter,* 8-9.

In Hitler's mind Darwinism provided the moral justification for infanticide, euthanasia, genocide, and other policies that had been (and thankfully still are) considered immoral by more conventional moral standards. Evolution provided the ultimate goals of his policy: the biological improvement of the human species. ...

If evolution provided the ends, the Darwinian mechanism suggested the means: increase the population of the "most fit" people to displace others in the struggle for existence. In his zeal to speed up the evolutionary process, he promoted both artificial selection (eugenics) and *policies to intensify natural selection*. Competition and conflict would advance the cause of the stronger, more fit individuals and races. But so would killing off those individuals and races deemed inferior. Morality could not be determined by any codes of the past, but only by the effects it has on evolutionary progress.[133]

There is a prevalent belief in our culture that Hitler was some sort of possessed lunatic who acted arbitrarily, without any coherent philosophy under-girding his actions, but this is simply not true. It is, rather, the opposite of true. We should probably learn to take our histories from historians rather than biologists. As Pichot notes:

> "We should probably learn to take our histories from historians rather than biologists."

Hitler did not invent very much; in most cases he was content to take up ideas that were in the air and to pursue them to their logical conclusions. Euthanasia and profound meditation on 'lives not worth living'

---

133 Ibid., 215, emphasis added.

were commonplaces of the time—and not only in Germany, even if the Nazis made great use of them and conducted propaganda around this theme. More or less all countries, in Europe and the United States, saw organizations campaigning for the legalization of Euthanasia. This was inspired by a kind of symmetry: eugenics (good birth) and euthanasia (good death) were the conditions for a good life—more important than social and economic reforms.[134]

Prior to the world wars, eugenics practices were pervasive throughout the western world. In fact, according to the sociologist Stephen Kuhl, "no other country played such a prominent role in Nazi propaganda" as the United States, and American eugenicists "were the strongest foreign supporters of Nazi race policies."[135]

To show its support for natural selection, the United States passed laws prohibiting marriage among the mentally handicapped, mentally ill, alcoholics and criminals as early as 1896 (Connecticut). By 1914, some 30 states had marriage prohibition laws on the books.[136] Between 1907 and 1913, beginning with Indiana, some 33 states passed laws providing for mandatory and compulsory sterilization.[137] The United States Supreme Court ruled in 1916 and again in 1927 in favor of compulsory sterilization, targeting criminals and the mentally handicapped, arguing that, "It is better for all the world if instead of waiting to execute degenerate offspring for crime, or to let them starve for their imbecility, society can prevent those who are manifestly *unfit* from continuing their kind."[138]

America did not oppose the German extermination of the weak and sick, and in fact, the cultural climate in the United States was obviously heading in precisely the same direction under the influence of the teleological interpretation of Darwinism. The division came only when the Nazis

---

134 Pichot, *The Pure Society*, 208.
135 Kuhl, *The Nazi Connection*, 37.
136 Pichot, *The Pure Society*, 150.
137 Ibid., 150-151.
138 Quoted in Kuhl, *The Nazi Connection*, 38, emphasis added.

redirected the eugenics program toward the Jews, where American racism had taken a decidedly different direction. According to Pichot:

> Without this extension [of the eugenics program to the Jews], no one would have had any complaint about the program, which before the war was broadly accepted, at least in its 'moderate' form of the sterilization of 'genetically incorrect' individuals, the segregation or sterilization of races categorized by science as 'inferior', and sometimes even the 'euthanasia' of individuals whose life 'was not worth living'.

"One can only shudder to think what the outcome would have been had German and American eugenicists coordinated their respective breeds of racism a bit better."

… this refocusing of the history of Nazism on anti-semitism has been a complete obfuscation of the logic of Nazi exterminations.

This has gone along with what we could call a Hollywoodizing of the extermination of the Jews. This extermination, in other words, has been framed and lit in such a way as to appear to be an isolated object, with well-defined, sharp contours against an obscure and vague background. The consequence of this has been to wipe out the historical context, left out of the frame or placed in shadow–a context that does not of course excuse the crime, but that at least partly explains its origins. …[139]

---

139 Pichot, *The Pure Society*, 329.

According to Pichot, Germans frequently looked upon Jews as the "white races bastardized by their contact with southern peoples, including Negroes,"[140] in which case, as we have already seen, they could summon a whole host of Darwinian biologists, physiologists, zoologists, ethnologists, etc., to concur that they were a genetically inferior quasi-human sub-species. One can only shudder to think what the outcome would have been had German and American eugenicists coordinated their respective breeds of racism a bit better.

There were between 350,000 and 400,000 compulsory sterilizations in Germany between 1934 and 1945.[141] Estimates of Nazi exterminations of the mentally and physically ill, the mentally and physically handicapped, and the elderly range from 70,000 to 275,000.[142] Over 6 million Jews and over 1 million children were systematically murdered due to their presumed biological inferiority. All told, the Holocaust claimed some 11 million lives.[143]

---

140 Ibid., 312.
141 Ibid., 191.
142 cf. Pichot, *The Pure Society,* 197-205.
143 Current estimates of human abortion in the past 50 years range from one to two billion souls. Abortion was common in the ancient world, but had been a punishable offense in the West throughout the Christian era.

Post-War Ateleology

The vast majority of the contemporary literature on the subject of ethics from the perspective of Naturalism is descriptive rather than prescriptive, and retrospective rather than prospective. This is, of course, the contemporary ateleological[144] response to the less-consistent teleological ethic of the eugenics movement.

We are frequently taken on guided tours of various groups of contemporary tribesmen whose ethical practices are assumed to resemble the practices of man in his evolutionary past, back in a time in which man was a little less human and a little more animal. We discover how these contemporaries of ours deal with deviant, aberrant members, and how shaming, the threat of banishment, etc., can be powerful and compelling incentives for man to quickly fall into line with the moral principles of his respective culture. Thus by studying these less-evolved folk, we learn–comically–how ethics are born out of the evolutionary swamp of today. Little to nothing is offered by way of ethical prescriptions, and, in the end, we are left with the inescapable impression that Naturalists just aren't confident about whether Naturalism has anything meaningful to say about ethics. To merely point out the obvious, this total absence of any clear prescriptive ethic must be seen as a pronounced deficiency and a conspicuous weakness of the philosophy of Naturalism as a whole. Knowledge is always unto wisdom

---

144 By "ateleological," I simply mean non-teleological.

and any system that doesn't help us to better inform our practice must be discarded as useless sophistry.

Furthermore, allowing that the contemporary perspective is quite obviously the retactionary antithesis of the eugenic thesis, it is very difficult to approach it without a measure of suspicion. First, upon what basis could the contemporary Naturalist renounce the eugenics movement as unethical? By what moral yardstick is he to judge the matter? He may pronounce it inconsistent with itself, of course, but still he has no basis upon which to renounce it as in any way *wrong*. A Naturalist might respond that renouncing the Holocaust as wrong falls clearly within the bounds of common sense, but then he must at least give some account as to why the old Darwinists

> Darwinian Naturalism is a comprehensive system of thought that explains what we are, where we came from, and where we stand in relation to all others. As such, it will inevitably determine our interpretation of our own worth, and the relative worth of all of the creatures and organisms around us.

didn't seem to have any common sense. Secondly, Darwinian Naturalism is a comprehensive system of thought that explains *what we are, where we came from*, and *where we stand in relation to all others*. As such, it will inevitably determine our interpretation of our own worth, and the relative worth of all of the creatures and organisms around us. Ethics and metaphysics can never be neatly isolated from one another, and so the view that Naturalism has no positive affirmations about ethics simply cannot be taken seriously. Given that the Naturalist of today disagrees entirely with the Naturalist of yesteryear about what those ethical implications *are*, how are we to be sure who is actually closer to the truth? It could, after all, reasonably be argued that today's Naturalist has the bias of the War and of the Holocaust behind him, and he is sure to be likened to Hitler and canned from his gig if he starts talking about helping natural selection along. The Naturalist of yesteryear, on the other hand, was far less impeded by the demands of culture and was much more free to see his program through.

As we have repeatedly seen, Naturalism occupies a precarious position with respect to teleology, as the non-teleological process of natural selection begets creatures like us whose thinking bears an indelible teleological imprint. In fact, upon examination, all of the basic terminology of Darwinism presupposes teleology at some level. *Adaptation* supposes some end to adapt unto. The *struggle for survival* is a struggle *for* survival. Common notions such as *fitness, progress, design, improvement*, etc. all very obviously presuppose teleology. Even *natural selection*, at a minimum, seems to imply that some *selection* is being done in accordance with some criteria (and the notion of "criteria" presupposes some end in view). The common response, of course, is that it merely *appears* to us to be teleological given that we are teleological creatures, but if this type of illusory pseudo-teleology[145] is permitted in our metaphysics and science, how consistent is it really to demand that we banish pseudo-teleology from our ethics?[146]

> "Rationality itself, at some level, presupposes teleology. To reason at all, you have to have a reason to reason."

---

145 Recently, pseudo-teleology has been spotted under the *pseudo*nyms "teleonomic" or "teleonomy," as if calling it by a new name would mitigate the problem.

146 It's interesting, in this connection, that Dawkins recently called it "immoral" to not abort a baby with down's syndrome (Twitter, August 20th, 2014, 10:53 am). Make no mistake; in a mere moment, the so-called freedom-of-choice will become the freedom-not-to-do-otherwise.

As we come to the end of our skyscraper tour, we find ourselves inching ever closer toward the conclusion that all human thought is inherently teleological, that rationality itself, at some level, presupposes teleology. To reason at all, you have to have a *reason* to reason. We're always reasoning for some reason, and no one ever reasons without having any reason at all for reasoning. We are decision-makers and problem-solvers; every decision supposes the weighing of objectives with respect to some end, and every problem supposes an obstacle to be overcome unto some end. Our metaphysical systems, for example, are aimed at interpreting the universe, in which case, the whole enterprise of philosophy is an inherently teleological enterprise, a sort of advanced problem-solving strategy. Likewise, the scientific enterprise is inherently teleological, as observation is always unto some end, and experimentation is always unto some end. Every scientific experiment is a teleological event, inasmuch as the scientist has some clear objective in mind. As all of the rest of our enterprises, science is a *purposeful* enterprise. There can be no *purposeless rationality*, and thus, rationality presupposes teleology. The notion of an unguided, purposeless thought is practically unthinkable, and even if there could be such a thought, it would certainly not be a particularly *rational* thought.

It will not really come as a surprise then that our thoughts about ethics will necessarily be of a teleological sort. To the extent that a person chooses one thing over another, or considers one course of action more desirable than another course of action, he has some *telos* or end in view. Even the refusal to act is a sort of negative election unto some perceived desirable end. Every code of conduct and principle of action, therefore, has a teleological shade to it, as every law and every human action presupposes a value-hierarchy in which, in the framework of some system, some things are viewed as *more valuable* than others. The squashing of a bug says something about the relative value of the bug from the perspective of the squasher. If, within the parameters of his metaphysic, the squasher believed that the bug was his grandmother or a god named Gozer, he would obviously act very differently toward it. These types of teleological value-hierarchies arise as a product of our own metaphysical systems. If, for example, we consider the value placed upon the cow within the framework of Hinduism and contrast this with the value of the cow within a Christian framework, and then think about how this works itself out in practice (e.g., one gazillion served), this point will be fairly obvious. In a Darwinian Naturalist scheme, the most obvious contenders for the highest conceivable *value* are human survival, the process of evolution, and the prerequisites of the process of evolution. Take a look at Dawkins' value-hierarchy:

> Living organisms exist for the benefit of DNA rather than the other way around. This won't be obvious yet, but I hope to persuade you of it. The messages that DNA molecules contain are all but eternal when seen against the time scale of individual lifetimes. The lifetimes of DNA messages (give or take a few mutations) are measured in units ranging from millions of years to hundreds of millions of years; or, in other words, ranging from 10,000 individual lifetimes to a trillion individual lifetimes. Each individual organism should be seen as a temporary vehicle, in which DNA messages spend a tiny fraction of the geological lifetimes.[147]

Dawkins' conception here, on the face of it anyway, is teleological. To say that "living organisms exist for the benefit of DNA" is to assume that there is some objective hierarchy of values within nature and that the cosmos assigns relative importance to things, apparently upon the basis of their relative staying-power and persistence. I exist for something greater, namely, "for the benefit of DNA." The lifespan of DNA information is "all but eternal" when compared to the individual, and so it naturally has higher value than this or that particular host-vessel. Human evolutionary process can exist without any particular human, of course, but it cannot exist without the human DNA code. It's not so much then that I use DNA for survival

---

147 Dawkins, *The Blind Watchmaker*, 180.

as that DNA uses me for survival. (As to why DNA is in the business of survival, I suppose that's none of my business).

This presents an obvious logical dilemma inasmuch as nature does not have teleological values in a Naturalist scheme and that therefore all such value-assignments and value-judgments must be entirely arbitrary as far as nature (i.e., the objective, outside world) is concerned. Nevertheless, it will still be true that at the foundation of any human ethical practice (and indeed, of any human action whatsoever, including the act of thinking) lies the assignment of teleological value. The dilemma here is obvious. If Naturalism renounces teleology in nature in the relevant sense, then it must continue to endorse the view that nature has nothing to say about ethics, and—to this it must add—that nature has nothing to say *at all*. If, on the other hand, Naturalists somehow manage to carve out a bit of space for teleology in nature, then, in addition to the fact that we exist for the benefit of DNA and not the other way around, it should probably be added that natural selection does not favor DNA in general, but rather those strands of DNA which carry the good designs. We exist not just for the benefit of any-old-DNA, but for the most persistent, fittest DNA. From this point, once culture begins to drink deeply from the old well of evolutionary progress, then it's probably only a matter of time until that first white finger points in one direction or another and makes its natural selection as to which of the usual suspects has to go. The teleological notion of evolutionary progress is arguably inherent in the concept of natural selection, given that natural selection always tends toward progress from the human perspective and that the human perspective is the only perspective with which we humans can approach anything whatsoever.

In any event, Naturalism must renounce either teleology in nature or ateleology in nature. If the former, then we have come to the end of the matter, for all thought is inherently teleological, while nature is inherently ateleological and never the twain shall meet. If the latter, then it must be conceded that the teleological interpretation of ethics was a reasonable interpretation all along, at which point history is bound to repeat itself. In renouncing its past, Naturalism must thus also renounce its future. *All human thought is rational and teleological, and if the realm of nature is neither rational nor teleological, then nothing can be known about it, not in an objective sense anyway, not in the sense that science supposes. The great and persistent irony of Darwinian Naturalism is that it is a teleological system which renounces teleology!*

> "All human thought is rational and teleological, and if the realm of nature is neither rational nor teleological, then nothing can be known about it."

Christianity, on any account, offers a dramatically different interpretation of man, of man's relationship to nature, and of the relative value of the human person and every other creature. In the biblical context, man exists as the centerpiece of nature, granted authority by God to have dominion over the rest of creation, to prudently dispose of plants, animals, and everything else as he sees fit unto the preservation of his own life, all of course subserving the purpose of true religion in the scheme of redemptive history.[148] Man has an inherent objective worth infinitely higher than any

> "Human life is sacred, because God is sacred and human life is made in the image of God."

other element of creation, since mankind, and mankind only, is made in the peculiar image of God. Man is like God, and this likeness makes man objectively and eternally valuable. To murder is to deface God's likeness, to lie is to defraud God's likeness, adultery

---

148 It is sometimes objected that asserting the relative importance of man over nature leads to excesses and abuses of power, but, first of all, Naturalism, at present, doesn't even have a way of measuring whether abuses of power are more desirable than non-abuses of power, secondly, the greatest abuses of power in recorded history were clearly begotten of one variety of Dawinian Naturalism, and finally, the notion that the Christian view leads to excesses has simply never been demonstrated historically.

is to put one divine likeness into an unfaithful relationship with another divine likeness, and so forth. The Christian ethic presupposes inherent human worth, and the inherent worth of the human person derives ultimately from the inherent worth of Yahweh himself. Human life is sacred, because God is sacred and human life is made in the image of God. The weak, the sick, the helpless, the poor, the unborn, etc., just as surely possess the immortal image of God as the strong and able. The notion of prudent social assistance as we know it–helping the widow, giving to the poor, etc.–is Judeo-Christian in both historical origin and essential character.

It is a fair question, however, and it certainly deserves an answer, haven't racist deeds and acts of hatred and injustice often been committed in the name of the Christian religion? While it is unquestionably true that the Bible has frequently been used to endorse many forms of injustice, it must still be allowed that the Bible is a very big book in which a phrase or a verse yanked out of its context can be forced to condone practically anything. Hitler himself appealed to the Bible to justify the Holocaust, which has to strike us as somewhat problematic given that the Bible is a book written by Jews about a Jewish Messiah. Ultimately, the question in this case is whether the Holocaust was consistent or inconsistent with the general principles of the Bible itself. For example, the Holocaust certainly had an element of racism to it, but does the Bible endorse or condone racism? Don't take it from me, but rather go to the source and decide for yourself. Listen to Jesus contrast Jew and gentile. Listen to him, in the mode of his culture, call a Gentile woman an animal–a dog–and then listen to his joy as he proceeds to destroy that distinction–and racism–forever:

> And Jesus went away from there and withdrew to the district of Tyre and Sidon. And behold, a Canaanite woman from that region came out and was crying, "Have mercy on me, O Lord, Son of David; my daughter is severely oppressed by a demon." But he did not answer her a word. And his disciples came and begged him, saying, "Send her away, for she is crying out after

us." He answered, "I was sent only to the lost sheep of the house of Israel." But she came and knelt before him, saying, "Lord, help me." And he answered, "It is not right to take the children's bread and throw it to the dogs." She said, "Yes, Lord, yet even the dogs eat the crumbs that fall from their masters' table." Then Jesus answered her, "O woman, great is your faith! Be it done for you as you desire." And her daughter was healed instantly. (Matthew 15:21-28)

Jesus called her people "the dogs", and the woman understood, of course, what this implied in her own case. The woman accepted the title (in vs. 27) because she wanted more than anything for her daughter to be healed, and she knelt before the "Son of David," the Messiah that God had promised ages ago, the one who could make her hope a reality. The thing to note is that her assumptions about Jesus were–in Jesus' view–correct. Jesus saw that she had the right type of "faith" and to a "great" degree and so his hard subterfuge gave way to the warm reality. She had passed his test with flying colors and he rejoiced to invite her into the fellowship of faith. He took off the mask of cultural bigotry to expose a smiling if not sun-beaten face, as one who has found that which was lost after a long and diligent search.

God *created* all men *equal* and he offers forgiveness to all men through faith in his Son Jesus Christ.[149] It is offered to everyone "from every nation, from all tribes and peoples and languages,"[150] regardless of race or social status, regardless of the skeletons in the closet, apart from any money or any merit whatsoever, and the children of God–such as this faithful Gentile woman–are a homogeneous unity, not the lesser and greater children of God, not the superior and inferior, not the real family members and the bond-servants, but a single church and a single family. As one Christian brother put it:

---

149 This salvation is offered to all, to me and to you and to Dawkins and to Dennett, both of whom I cannot help but like a great deal, as they are good old fashioned absolutists like me!

150 Revelation 7:9 (Biblical citations are ESV unless otherwise noted).

I have a dream that one day "every valley shall be exalted, and every hill and mountain shall be made low, the rough places will be made plain, and the crooked places will be made straight; and the glory of the Lord shall be revealed and *all* flesh shall see it together." [Isaiah 40:4-5] This is our hope, and this is the faith that I go back to the South with. With this faith, we will be able to hew out of the mountain of despair a stone of hope. With this faith, we will be able to transform the jangling discords of our nation into a beautiful symphony of brotherhood. With this faith, we will be able to work together, to pray together, to struggle together, to go to jail together, to stand up for freedom together, *knowing* that we will be free one day.[151]

Racism is the belittling of the image of God to his face. A racist Christian is an inconsistent Christian, though we admit, of course, that there has been a great deal of inconsistency. Still, it is no argument against Christianity that Christians are hypocrites and sinners, for Christianity teaches exactly *that*. John Newton, the slave trader turned abolitionist, author of the hymn *Amazing Grace*, said it best near the end of his life: "My memory is nearly gone; but I remember two things: That I am a great sinner, and that Christ is a great Savior."[152] We have surely committed many evils and many wrongs, but yet even our wrongdoing presupposes that there is such a thing as *wrong*. There can be no world in which *everything is relative* and yet slavery and the like still be accounted *objectively wrong*. If everything is relative, then the wrongness of slavery is relative and there will be very little room for complaining when the cultural tide shifts again in its favor and it overtakes our children or our children's children.

Naturalism gets everything backwards; it rids the world of self-sacrifice, love, forgiveness, joy, and meaning, and replaces these with either the vacuum of relativity or with war, death, and suffering. And for what? For

151 Martin Luther King, Jr., "I have a Dream" speech, http://www.americanrhetoric.com/speeches/mlkihaveadream.htm, emphasis added.
152 http://www.reformedreader.org/rbb/newton/neindex.htm

some genetic material that will be gone in due time, in any event, on anyone's account, anyway? All of our efforts at self-preservation are, on a long enough time line, foredoomed to failure, in which case, if there is no God and no immortality, "Let us eat and drink, for tomorrow we die."[153] It is another profound curiosity–a curiosity of curiosities– that exalting the value of the human

> "Naturalism is a sort of task-master that, in order to gain assent in us, must first convince us that we are individually worthless."

genetic material leads inevitably to the debasement of all humanity. Naturalism is a sort of task-master that, in order to gain assent in us, must first convince us that we are individually worthless. I think we're worth more, and, in fact, I think we're worth much more. You are not an animal. "You are of more value," said Jesus, "than many sparrows."[154] You were not born out of some slime at random, but rather you have been "fearfully and wonderfully made."[155] Your life is not meaningless, but rather, you have endless objective significance.

Regarding ethics then, Naturalism doesn't work in practice, because it simply isn't true in principle. Christianity offers coherent rationality alongside systematic ethical practice, persistent meaning, and logically-justified personal satisfaction. As we have maintained for countless ages, even so now we maintain that Christianity works because it is true, where every other system is self-defeating in principle and constricting in practice. Christianity

---

153 1 Corinthians 15:32. In its context, the meaning seems to be that if there is no immortality and, therefore, no ultimate consequences to our deeds, we should cast off any and every ethical system and live for the day, given that the day is all that we have, and dead men have no regrets (assuming there is no immortality). Given the Christian understanding of the Bible, as a book written under the inspiration of the Holy Spirit, presumably this is God's take on the matter, God's opinion regarding this particular counter-factual scenario.

154 Matthew 10:31

155 Psalm 139:14

is rationality for man, which is to say there can be no true reasoning apart from faith, which is to say that, as it turns out, the fear of the Lord is still the beginning of wisdom. (Proverbs 9:10)[156]

---

156 The thing to note about fear is that the fear of God presupposes both the existence of God along with God's power to punish. The fear of the Lord, in other words, presupposes faith and is, in the context of the Bible, synonymous with faith–faith under the Old Testament veil.

The Apparent and the Actual

Naturalism is the orthodoxy of the academic community and the Saturday morning cartoon alike and, seemingly, there are very few viable alternatives and very little end in sight. To put it simply, when the supernatural is excluded, the natural is all that remains, and Naturalism wins by default.[157] From this perspective, it seems almost certain that the cultural dominance of Naturalism is just getting under way. A "certain amount of corrosive work has already been done by Darwin's dangerous idea, and can never be undone."[158] If it's cultural respectability or cutting-edge scholarship you're searching for in the open market of ideas, then I commend Naturalism to you as the obvious choice.

Still it is true, however, that to be consistent, the outlook of unguided evolution must apply the fact of change and of evolution back upon itself, thereby robbing itself of every last vestige of dignity and every last artifice of persistence and self-importance. Naturalism posits a world without *telos* or teleology, and thereby

> "When evolution evolves, it can evolve into the very opposite of itself given a long enough time line."

---

157 The natural/supernatural distinction is a faulty distinction of our culture. Nothing is so natural as God. We are the novel oddities and odd novelties in the world; God was here all along.
158 Dennett, *Darwin's Dangerous Idea*, 83.

instantly defines itself as meaningless and insignificant. It posits a world of unpredictable change, and thereby renders its own conclusions transient and untrue to the degree that such conclusions will certainly be rendered untrue eventually. It sets out on a purposeful search for rationality upon the premise that we live in a purposeless, non-rational world. Within the matrix of Naturalism, man is condemned to the sentence of life and forced to chase after mirages like meaning, value, and knowledge. The only thing that can withstand consistent Darwinism—the only survivor in the survival of the fittest—is that new fundamental feeling of conclusive transitoriness. When evolution evolves, it can evolve into the very opposite of itself given a long enough time line.

In light of the dissatisfying and hopeless picture of things that we find inside the skyscraper of Naturalism, perhaps you will deal with my foolishness for another moment or two—to endure a few more out-of-place movie references and ill-conceived jokes—in order to hear a few words about the Christian hope. If there is here a degree of emotional appeal, I can at least assure you I won't be asking you to abandon your rationality at any point along the way. We will merely continue with the theme that, among worldviews, Christianity offers the highest degree of explanatory power, and we shall try to focus that power a bit into the inward world of man.

As we have repeatedly seen, we all believe what we *want* to believe and it is also true that our commitments to our individual systems can never be neatly isolated from our feelings or moral inclinations. The American philosopher, Michael Rea, put it this way:

> So when it comes to rejecting one program in favor of another, the decision to adopt the favored program must be made on pragmatic grounds, broadly speaking, rather than evidential grounds. In such cases, one chooses the program whose consequences are most attractive, or whose canons are most convenient to adopt, or whose adoption will most irritate one's enemies, or whatever. Furthermore, even if it happens to be true

that (say) one rationally ought to adopt the program whose consequences are more attractive rather than the program whose adoption will most irritate one's enemies, there are no discernible grounds for asserting this truth. For, again, one could discern the grounds for asserting it *as grounds* for asserting it only within the context of some research program.[159]

Worldview selection, at this point, probably doesn't look quite as objective as it might have at the outset. On anyone's account, a lot of smart people believe a lot of dumb stuff. Far from being just cold and calculated number-crunching, choosing a system is probably much more like choosing a mate. You consider its relative attractiveness, to what degree it is compatible with you personally, to what extent it is likely to satisfy your needs and desires on into the future, and what sorts of personal sacrifices the commitment will cost you (if indeed you are committed). It's also easy to overlook the undesirable parts even if friends and family are kind enough to try to bring them to light. Love is blind indeed; we see what we want to see and we believe what we want to believe.

Most of us hold views that are only modestly different from those of our parents. (It's pretty much true in my case). Most of us really never gave it much thought; we just took it as it came to us from some presumed authority–that one minister or that one professor or that one episode on The Discovery Channel. In most cases, it was just that authority that happened to get to us first, whose outlook

> "Everyone seems to think that their science is final, even though the very notion of a final science runs contrary to the whole scientific enterprise."

159 Michael C. Rea, *World Without Design: The Ontological Consequences of Naturalism* (Oxford: Oxford University Press, 2002), 7.

rubbed off on us and seemed to help us interpret our own experience the next day and therefore seemed self-authenticating, like so much self-fulfilling prophecy. Everyone thinks they're not brainwashed, while yet suspecting that everyone else probably is. Everyone thinks they've learned "to think for themselves," while yet suspecting that everyone else merely

> "Some live closer than others, of course, but none of us lives squarely in the real world."

rests on the authority of some authority.[160] Every modern physicist laughs at Aristotle's account of physics as ancient superstition, while at the same time failing to recognize that his own views will soon enough be someone else's ancient superstition. Everyone seems to think that their science is *final*, even though the very notion of a *final science* runs contrary to the whole scientific enterprise. The foolish man, it seems, still builds his house upon the sand. Worse still is the fact that most of us hold views that are mostly incoherent and self-defeating. The average earthling today is an annoyance to consistent Naturalist and consistent Christian alike, for he is trapped somewhere in the middle, an ugly marriage of the natural selection theory with a bit of god-talk to putty up perceived gaps and give his life some semblance of persistence. In the free market of ideas, most of us just pick and choose *a la carte*. We point our compass in the direction of perceived comfort and satisfaction, grab a little of this and a little of that, and off we go. We pick the path of least resistance in pursuit of leisure and pleasure, the path that appears widest and easiest to us individually. Some live closer than others, of course, but none of us lives squarely in the real world.

If you're anything like me, you probably just want to sin in peace, without guilt or the fear of punishment. We're generally not trying to upset

---

160 And, with respect to our origin, what else is there? As Kuhn observed, "science students accept theories on the authority of teacher and text, not because of evidence. What alternatives have they, or what competence? The applications given in texts are not there as evidence but because learning them is part of learning the paradigm at the base of current practice." (Kuhn, *The Structure of Scientific Revolutions*, 79.)

anyone or to rock the boat, but precisely the opposite—we just want to be left alone to enjoy a little leisure and a little pleasure on our own terms, to be, as it were, the masters of our own domain. That being the case, the thing that sometimes strikes us as undesirable about God is just that he seems like a total drag and a big downer with all of the rules and the regulations and the threatenings. Who wants to be a part of all that? It all sounds abysmal really, more like a sacrifice of life than life itself, and here Naturalism can sometimes look like a very pleasant alternative. God and the fear of judgment are equally excluded, and if we hurt someone, we don't have to ask forgiveness if we don't feel like it, for we answer to no one but ourselves. We're just animals, after all, and nobody should really expect that much of us. If we foster a few bad habits, then probably nobody will find out, and probably nobody will get hurt, and even if they do, though it is sad that history will soon forget us, there is consolation at least in the fact that our bad deeds will be forgotten alongside all the others. Every commitment costs something, of course, and every commitment pays some dividends.

When you get right down to it though, there are still things that you haven't yet explained to your own satisfaction; there are seams that you notice, inconsistencies, inductive instances that keep you unsettled and that force you to keep searching. You search for rest but still you are restless. Though God and the fear of judgment are excluded in principle, still you have lingering and unshakable feelings of shame, isolation, abandonment, and a certain detestable sense of guilt, as if you owed yourself something more, and as if you owed someone else something more. You remind yourself often that these feelings are unreal, just cultural constructs, or evolutionary waste, or faulty parenting (or something), and you get frustrated with yourself that you cannot force heart and conscience to submit to the demands of logic and will. Yet those unreal feelings still feel viscerally and despicably real. Creatures who have spent millions of years in the evolutionary mill should really have much thicker skin than you and I have.

Have you embraced the certain prospect of being forgotten forever after living an objectively meaningless life involving a few objectively meaningless relationships and perhaps an objectively meaningless child or two? I'd venture to guess that you have a few guilty pleasures tucked away somewhere, a few delusions about this or that somehow being significant, even though you really should know better by now. Everyone looks for immortality somewhere, in progeny or fame or something else. God has set eternity in the heart of man.[161] The search for immortality is basic to us, for *significance* with an expiration date has never struck anyone as particularly significant. We've become increasingly isolated inside of our earbuds mostly just because it still sounds like they're getting worked up about something meaningful in there, as if they've managed to escape the world in which the engineering marvels and scientific achievements of man will all add up to nothing in the end. You live as if your life has lasting significance and you cannot live consistently upon the premise that this is all there is.

Still, Christianity is a hard pill to swallow. It's difficult to take Jesus seriously when he tells us that sin is slavery, objectively considered.[162] It sounds like straight-forward nonsense to say that doing what you want to do is slavery, and doing what someone else wants you to do is freedom. It has all the appearances of a lie–and a very superficial lie at that–but still, nobody really wants to bad-mouth Jesus, and so maybe it deserves a second look. Personally, I think it's something like what Tyler Durden taught us about material possessions, that, though it was precisely the opposite of what you intended, "the things you own end up owning you."[163]

I propose a simple test. Here is how you test the slavery hypothesis for yourself. All of us have habits that we're not particularly proud of, that we try to hide from most people most of the time, that we're unwilling to give up and, if we're being honest, that we can't give up. We all do things that we would advise our children not to do. Why is it that we harbor these sorts of embarrassments and inconsistencies? We're certainly not in the market for self-respect, personal integrity, or social standing, and so probably the

---

161 Ecclesiastes 3:11
162 "Jesus answered them, "Truly, truly, I say to you, everyone who practices sin is a slave to sin. The slave does not remain in the house forever; the son remains forever. So if the Son sets you free, you will be free indeed." (John 8:34-36)
163 Fight Club, David Fincher, 20th Century Fox, 1999…sir.

answer is that we're looking to reap a measure of personal satisfaction from our bad habits. If that's roughly true in your particular case, then presumably the relevant question is, simply, how is it working for you? Perhaps consider just the most obvious of your sins. Probably something has already sprung to mind. How much stress does it cause you? How frequently do you worry about it? How much time do you spend sowing the seeds of satisfaction and how much time do you spend reaping the satisfaction itself? You have to answer the question for yourself, and you have to have the decency to consider it for a time and to try not to trick yourself: if you were to weigh your satisfaction in sin against your stress from sin, which would be the heavier?

> Thus says the LORD of hosts: Consider your ways. You have sown much, and harvested little. You eat, but you never have enough; you drink, but you never have your fill. You clothe yourselves, but no one is warm. And he who earns wages does so to put them into a bag with holes. You looked for much, and behold, it came to little ... And when you brought it home, I blew it away. (Haggai 1:5-6,9)[164]

Think back to the garden. You know the plot. Adam and Eve ate of the fruit expecting wisdom. They interpreted the Tree from the perspective of a faulty framework, and their expectations were confounded. They sought for life and wisdom but found only death. Ever since that time it has been true that nothing sounds quite so dreadful to us as *obedience* and nothing seems to hold so much promise as *forbidden fruit*, but perhaps our ears are playing some sort of trick on us here? *Anxiety* and *uncertainty* entered the world in precisely that moment in which Eve began to weigh the testimony and authority of God against the competing testimony and authority of the serpent, the moment she began to contemplate a departure from the true system of God, which was all she had known up until that point, an integral

---

164 The context is that the Israelites were going about their business while the temple lay in disrepair. They had failed to concern themselves about the things of God, as evidenced by the temple ruins.

part of the original design. We likewise set our compass in the direction of perceived satisfaction in sin and we take the quickest and easiest route to get there, and yet, in the end, it is as the carrot on the end of a string, the promises unfulfilled, the expectation confounded.

Understand this: sin will never satisfy you, because you were designed to be satisfied by something much greater. You have grossly underestimated your own significance; you are much too important to be satisfied with such trifles. Satisfaction in sin would be contrary to the very structure of the entire design, contrary to your Creator's program entirely. No wonder then you've been paying for a pound and only getting an ounce.

Toil here with me another moment. According to the Apostle Peter, God himself is an active participant in your unshakeable discontent:

> the Lord knows how to rescue the godly from trials, *and to keep the unrighteous under punishment until the day of judgment,* and especially those who indulge in the lust of defiling passion and despise authority. (2 Peter 2: 9-10 emphasis added)

This seems dastardly, of course–downright abominable–that the very hand of Omnipotence is set against you, thoroughly overseeing your individual case, maintaining your *punishment*, as it were, weighing down your spirit, blowing away your happiness without notice or consent, determining certainly that you will never achieve your goal of finding lasting satisfaction or peace apart from him, but here we have to stop again and rehearse again our developing theme that appearances can be misleading and that there is something *fundamentally backwards* about the way you and I look at things. Adam and Eve tried to get it to work in a way in which it was not designed to work, and the apple, as they say, does not fall far from the tree.[165] In the moment that it annoys you that God concerns himself with your personal business, you've missed the real point entirely, namely, that *God* concerns

---

165 "Therefore, just as through one man sin entered into the world, and death through sin, and so death spread to all men, because all sinned ..." (Romans 5:12)

himself with your personal business. The all-knowing, all-powerful Creator of the universe has some strange interest in you. Why? Because he's bored? Because he's vindictive? Because you're so engaging? No, he concerns himself with your personal business because he's concerned about your person and about you personally. Not all punishment is vengeance, of course; a good father punishes not out of spite but to protect his children, to keep them from harming themselves, to begin them on the path of self-discipline and integrity. Our heavenly Father is the archetype, paradigm, and precondition of all fathers, of course, "we are indeed his offspring,"[166] and fatherly discipline, when done well, when viewed objectively, is a profound blessing and a great kindness. That being the case, you should consider "that God's kindness is meant to lead you to repentance"[167] just as you should also consider the possibility that sin really is some sort of blind love and self-imposed slavery.

Don't misunderstand me though; I'm not in any way suggesting that you need to stop searching for satisfaction, or for leisure and pleasure. Quite to the contrary, I'm suggesting that you need to look for them much harder and that, so far, you've been looking in entirely the wrong place. Consider, if only for a moment, the ontological source and wellspring of all satisfaction, of all pleasure and all happiness and all joy and of every other good thing. Whence does it come? From whom do these derive their origin? "Every good gift and every perfect gift is from above, coming down from the Father of lights with whom there is no variation or shadow due to change."[168] Here is a good and loving Father who does not evolve at all and who always delights in giving gifts. My own conviction is that he designed you for worship, and, as a great mastermind, so too he designed you to be most satisfied *by* worship. No better design is conceivable than "an equilibrium where prevalence is a non-singular event where nobody loses."[169] Understand that I'm not just talking about a distant next life, I'm talking about here and now as well. I'm talking about a testable experiential hypothesis. His joy and your joy,

---

166 Acts 17:28 (Paul is quoting a Greek author while speaking to a Greek audience).
167 Romans 2:4
168 James 1:17
169 A Beautiful Mind, Ron Howard, Universal Pictures, 2002.

his satisfaction and your satisfaction, do not run in opposite directions as you've been thinking, but rather his satisfaction and your satisfaction, his happiness and your happiness, join up at precisely the same place–in the moment of praise. "The chief end of man is to glorify God by enjoying him forever."[170] Pleasing him pleases us, by design, and true freedom, on this account, is judging correctly from the vantage of the correct system. Where obedience formerly *appeared* ugly, and the forbidden fruit of sin seemed to be life itself and life to the fullest, a change of perspective reveals that there is *actually* great suffering in sin, and unspeakable joy in knowing God and in recognizing God's law as the reflection and image of the character of God himself:

> Oh how I love your law!
> It is my meditation all the day.
> Your commandment makes me wiser than my enemies,
> for it is ever with me.
> I have more understanding than all my teachers,
> for your testimonies are my meditation.
> I understand more than the aged,
> for I keep your precepts.
> I hold back my feet from every evil way,
> in order to keep your word.
> I do not turn aside from your rules,
> for you have taught me.
> How sweet are your words to my taste,
> sweeter than honey to my mouth! (Psalm 119:97-103)

Another way of saying the same thing is that true freedom is getting precisely what you want when what you want is precisely what will satisfy you the most. The addict defines freedom as appeasing his addiction, but

---

170 John Piper, *Desiring God: Meditations of a Christian Hedonist* (Portland: Multnomah. 1986), 14. (paraphrasing The Westminster Shorter Catechism, question 1).

everyone else can see that he is, in reality, a self-deceived slave on the path of self-destruction. We likewise hold onto sin like it's some sort of life preserver, oblivious to the fact that the sin we cherish is made of lead and chained to our ankle. We come to embrace and to value the very source of our misery while simultaneously shunning the God who designed us to be consummately satisfied in him. To deny God, after all, is to deny what you yourself *are* and, indeed, to deny your very own possibility and precondition, as the computer denying the existence of man. To know yourself, you must know him, and to deny him, you must also deny yourself. Every vain effort to construct an imaginary world in which God does not exist is marked to its very core by frustration and suffering, for the denial of God is the *de facto* denial of self. You're starving yourself to death, because you've come to believe good food is bad for you. I'm suggesting, on the other hand, that there is a way to gain satisfaction both in this life and the next, by sacrificing the delusion that your sin is going to satisfy you here *any day now*. Where nothing else can work, the truth will work, and it will indeed set you free from the slavery of sin, and from the weighty and manifold sufferings that always come right alongside.[171] You and I need a new perspective entirely;

> To deny God, after all, is to deny what you yourself are and, indeed, to deny your very own possibility and precondition, as the computer denying the existence of man. To know yourself, you must know him, and to deny him, you must also deny yourself.

---

171 I do not intend to imply that a Christian can ever become sinless. Though the Christian has a new moral compass, sin still persists. Righteousness grows over time and sin wanes over time in the Christian, a gradual transformation that is completed only when we meet Jesus face to face (cf. 1 John, esp. 3:2-3).

it's not so much "get busy living, or get busy dying"[172] as it is get busy doing both: to live to God and to die to sin,[173] to take off the old self and to put on a brand new self.[174] You must lay aside finite perspectives and authorities in favor of the infinite perspective and steadfast authority of God.

Every commitment costs something, of course. So what is God asking? What is the price of admission? You'll have to bear with me another moment here. He's asking for nothing short of moral perfection and perfect obedience to his every commandment from the moment of your birth until the moment of your death. He is righteous and holy in every aspect,[175] he will not have long-term fellowship with sinners,[176] and he will not flinch or bend or compromise on this point even one micron. He is not in the business of accommodating himself to our poor standards of what constitutes a "good person," and it must be admitted that if we take each individual's word for it, only good people live on this planet. You don't even meet your own ethical standards—you condemn the one who lies to you, though you frequently lie—and so it shouldn't be that surprising really that you don't meet the ethical standards of God.[177] Now you understand intuitively that this is bad news, because you understand intuitively that you have not met this standard. You understand intuitively that you have fallen short of this perfect fulfillment of God's law. You understand intuitively, in other words, that you are a sinner in God's world.[178] "Nobody's perfect" is condemnation of us all. It may be

---

172 The Shawshank Redemption, Frank Darabont, Castle Rock Entertainment, 1994.

173 "Now if we died with Christ, we believe that we will also live with him. For we know that since Christ was raised from the dead, he cannot die again; death no longer has mastery over him. The death he died, he died to sin once for all; but the life he lives, he lives to God. In the same way, count yourselves dead to sin but alive to God in Christ Jesus. Therefore do not let sin reign in your mortal body so that you obey its evil desires. Do not offer any part of yourself to sin as an instrument of wickedness, but rather offer yourselves to God as those who have been brought from death to life; and offer every part of yourself to him as an instrument of righteousness. For sin shall no longer be your master ..." (Romans 6:8-14)

174 "You were taught, with regard to your former way of life, to put off your old self, which is being corrupted by its deceitful desires; to be made new in the attitude of your minds; and to put on the new self, created to be like God in true righteousness and holiness." (Ephesians 4:22-24)

175 cf. 1 John 1:5

176 cf. Isaiah 59:2

177 "Do you suppose, O man—you who judge those who practice such things and yet do them yourself—that you will escape the judgment of God?" (Romans 2:3)

178 cf. Romans 1

some consolation, however, that this is very bad news not just for you but for me too and for every other imperfect person around here. You understand, of course, that it follows logically that if there is to be any hope for anyone at all, we need this moral perfection somehow from the outside, as a sort of stamp on the hand indicating that the price of admission has been paid in full. Personally, I'm desperate for some good news for a change:

> But now the righteousness of God has been manifested apart from the law, although the Law and the Prophets bear witness to it—the righteousness of God through faith in Jesus Christ for all who believe. For there is no distinction [between Jews and gentiles]: for all have sinned and fall short of the glory of God, and are justified by his grace as a gift, through the redemption that is in Christ Jesus, whom God put forward as a propitiation [or appeasement] by his blood, to be received by faith. This was to show God's righteousness ... so that he might be just and the justifier of the one who has faith in Jesus. (Romans 3:21-26)

The asking price is faith (i.e., trust) in Christ in exchange for the overflowing superabundance of the righteousness of Christ and a *permanent* sinless *legal* standing before God. The apostle Paul here is not talking about x number of good deeds beforehand, he's not talking about straightening yourself up first, or making x number of appearances at church first, but a righteousness "apart from the law," that is, apart from your personal obedience to God's commandments, externally stamped on the hand, or, if you like, unalterably and irrevocably implanted in the chest, as a new heart of flesh replacing the old heart of stone.[179] Paul is talking about the "gift" of *imputed* righteousness upon the condition of *fidelity*[180] to the Son of God, the Lamb who laid down his life for the sins of the world. He's talking

---

179 And I will give you a new heart, and a new spirit I will put within you. And I will remove the heart of stone from your flesh and give you a heart of flesh. (Ezekiel 36:26)

180 The idea of a blind "leap of faith" is simply a modern-day fiction. Faith is the opposite of unfaithfulness. Faith is commitment to God in light of the certainty of his promises.

about what theologians call "substitutionary atonement" or, to say the same thing, "justification by faith alone," the cornerstone of Christian religion. The good news—the *gospel*—is that you can have everlasting peace with God and the renewal of true satisfaction starting this very instant, if you would only believe.

There's always a catch, of course. As you study your Bible and begin to think God's thoughts after him and to adopt the divine perspective, so to speak, from one degree to another heading on into the future, you're bound to look at sin differently and you're bound to act differently toward it, but that's really only to say that, heading on into the future, you will inevitably find more satisfaction in God and his righteousness than you ever did in sin.

Now the "transfer of allegiance from paradigm to paradigm is a conversion experience that cannot be forced"[181] and it will surely be rejected if it's not sincere, but it doesn't have to be perfect either. Hesitation, confusion, and even a measure of disbelief are okay. You wouldn't be the first or the last to cry out to God "I believe; help my unbelief!"[182] The most important point is that you *do* cry out.

The truth is that he has blessed you in countless ways, and you have not been very grateful. My running-water sink is greater than Solomon's whole kingdom, to say nothing of the garbage disposal. The truth is that he's been looking after you, and that you resented him for it, that he has been gentle with you while you were plotting your escape and his destruction. The truth is that you read *his* Bible on *your* terms, and you were content to note some inconsistencies somewhere in the mix and to move on. The truth is that even the minor offenses are major offenses, and that the smallest of your sins is nothing short of cosmic treason and insurrection against your very Creator, for which you deserve death and much worse, yet the Lamb of God died the death of a criminal to take the place of criminals like you and me. The very same one from whom you have been running—the very same

---

181 (In context, Kuhn is talking about switching from one scientific paradigm to another). Kuhn, *The Structure of Scientific Revolutions*, 151.

182 Mark 9:24

one against whom you have sinned–has himself bridged the gap to make you whole, though you must grab hold of him!

> He was oppressed, and he was afflicted,
> yet he opened not his mouth;
> like a lamb that is led to the slaughter,
> and like a sheep that before its shearers is silent,
> so he opened not his mouth.
> By oppression and judgment he was taken away;
> and as for his generation, who considered
> that he was cut off out of the land of the living,
> *stricken for the transgression of my people?*
> And they made his grave with the wicked
> and with a rich man in his death,
> although he had done no violence,
> and there was no deceit in his mouth.
> Yet it was the will of the LORD to crush him;
> he has put him to grief;
> when his soul makes an offering for guilt,
> he shall see his offspring; he shall prolong his days;
> the will of the LORD shall prosper in his hand.
> Out of the anguish of his soul he shall see and be satisfied;
> by his knowledge shall the righteous one, my servant,
> *make many to be accounted righteous,*
> *and he shall bear their iniquities.*
> Therefore I will divide him a portion with the many,
> and he shall divide the spoil with the strong,
> because he poured out his soul to death
> and was numbered with the transgressors;
> *yet he bore the sin of many,*
> and makes intercession for the transgressors. (Isaiah 53:7-12 emphasis added)

The "righteous one" had to suffer and die as a criminal in order for the many to be "accounted righteous." That seems to be precisely what we're talking about here, and so it's probably worth pointing out that the prophet Isaiah penned these words some 700 years prior to the birth of Christ. We still have manuscripts of the book which predate the birth of Christ by over a century. Go see it with your own eyes.[183] That's a terrific conspiracy, isn't it? An epic coincidence? This much is certain–there is some great mastermind behind all of this somewhere.

You probably noticed something strange in the middle there though, that it was the will of God to crush him? That God the Father turned his back on his Son for the first time ever, after existing for an eternity before that, having never done so before, and that he went into this whole business willfully?[184] What could that all be about? What motivation could an unchanging God possibly have for that sort of nonsense, or, for that matter, for creating any of this in the first place? That's not an easy question, of course, but here's a relatively straight-forward answer, and you can judge for yourself whether it's any good or not. For the Father, his love for his Son would be magnified forever, both retrospectively and prospectively, against the backdrop of this one moment of suffering. The Father undoubtedly suffered as he turned his back on his Son for the first time, as he turned away from the horror of my sin, now imputed momentarily to his only-begotten. He suffered on his own behalf and–no doubt–he suffered even more on his Son's behalf. He is righteous though. If he is *anything*, he is righteous, and he must shun that which tends unto the disgrace or destruction of his own image, and hence, he hates evil, and hence, he turned away from this atrocity of atrocities, this host of holocausts heaped upon his Son. Yet in the midst of infinite pain the Father kept one eye on certain victory; he knew that just as surely as the sun would rise again, his Son would rise again, and, to speak with figure, that he would greet him again with open arms and that he would squeeze him again tightly into his chest, with a world won and

---

183 http://dss.collections.imj.org.il/isaiah
184 cf. Acts 2:23, Matthew 27:46

nothing whatsoever lost between them. As a proud Father, he will honor the victory of his Son over sin and death on the cross *forever*. And for the Son? That one's easier. He bore the pain in order to redeem for himself a people,[185] to glorify his Father, and in order to achieve the very same retrospective and prospective[186] magnification of his Father's love.[187] "For the joy that was set before him [he] endured the cross."(Hebrews 12:2)

As to his being, God does not change, not at all, never evolves, never discovers. Whatever happens, he saw it coming all along. Still, the Son of God, who has existed forever as God, became irrevocably united with a brand new human person around 3 B.C. in order to accomplish human redemption, being uniquely situated–as the Son of God and the Son of Man–to bring God and man back into fellowship with one another. That being the case, while it is true that God does not change with respect to his *character* or *being*, still it is obviously true that God *does* change with respect to his *actions, emotions,* and *external relations*. Before he spoke it into being, there was no universe, of course, and in creation God enters into new relationships, relationships that did not *actually* exist prior to that point, though they certainly did exist in his mind's eye, so to speak. Here's what I'm getting at: God loves himself because he's three selves, a sort of unfolding reflection of himself,[188] Father, Son, and Spirit, and though men do not understand it very well, women understand that you can always find some new way to express your love. The cross was a momentary pause in the never-ending chorus of divine self-love (tempered, of course, by the certain foreknowledge of how it would all turn out) and the cross of Christ tended ultimately unto the magnification of that self-love, unto the glory of God forever.

---

185 cf. Titus 2:14

186 I mean retrospective in the sense that he saw it coming all along, that he has foreknowledge of everything, and prospective in the sense that these events actually happened at a particular moment in time, i.e., that God cannot honor the victory of his Son on the cross in the fullest sense until after such victory has actually occurred.

187 Of the Holy Spirit's role in the economy of redemption, I have written elsewhere. (The second edition of my book on the Trinity is forthcoming.)

188 The Son is the only-begotten (the Greek is *"mono-genes"*; if you remember what *eu-genes* meant, this one is easy enough to decipher) "image" or "form" or "imprint" or facsimile of his Father, and the Spirit is the image of both Father and Son. Cf. Philippians 2:6, Hebrews 1:3, Colossians 1:13-15, 2 Corinthians 4:4. Also see the Nicene Creed and footnote 187.

In creation, God stamped the image of himself upon man, a new image in the likeness of the old image, but man deformed the image in the fall. In salvation, God renews the image in the likeness of the Lamb by the power of the Holy Spirit, God adopts the image as his child through faith,[189] from one degree of glory to another,[190] and God weaves his love for his Son into the narrative of someone's life, right here upon the canvas of history.

The Lamb of God died because of sin that we too might die to sin, to walk, as it were, in his footsteps and image, as righteous, even as he himself walked in the manner of his Father. "He himself bore our sins in his body on the tree, that we might die to sin and live to righteousness."[191] He rose from the dead so that we might live once again unto the Father instead of being stuck down in the mire of sin and death. "For our sake he made him to be sin who knew no sin, so that in him we might become the righteousness of God."[192] The Son of God rose like a dead man, that we dead men might arise from the dead to be adopted as sons, the image replicated, the brand new children of God, "and if children, then heirs—heirs of God and fellow heirs with Christ,"[193] an extended family, caught up in the chorus of divine love forever.

The Lamb of God died as a sacrifice to take away the sins of the world[194] and it is this Lamb that you must pause now to consider. It is this Lamb that you must not merely avoid as usual, but to grab hold of and to wrestle with, as Israel in the days of old![195] It is this Lamb you must embrace as God and pronounce as risen, or reject as history's most brilliant liar, just another dead guy whose bones are rotting out there in a field somewhere. It is this Lamb who stands–by design–at the axis of history calling all men unto himself as the lighthouse of the universe, inviting the masses in for

---

189 cf. Romans 8:15, 23, 9:4, Galatians 4:5, Ephesians 1:5

190 "And we all, with unveiled face, beholding the glory of the Lord, are being transformed into the same image from one degree of glory to another. For this comes from the Lord who is the Spirit." (2 Corinthians 3:18)

191 1 Peter 2:24

192 2 Corinthians 5:21

193 Romans 8:17

194 The next day [John the baptist] saw Jesus coming toward him, and said, "Behold, the Lamb of God, who takes away the sin of the world!" (John 1:29)

195 See Genesis 32.

his supper, in for *shalom*, for complete fellowship with complete peace and satisfaction completely without shame or fear. It is this Lamb who came to bring healing and rest to his sick and weak lost sheep:

> At that time Jesus declared, "I thank you, Father, Lord of heaven and earth, that you have hidden these things from the wise and understanding and revealed them to little children; yes, Father, for such was your gracious will. All things have been handed over to me by my Father, and no one knows the Son except the Father, and no one knows the Father except the Son and anyone to whom the Son chooses to reveal him. Come to me, all who labor and are heavy laden, and I will give you rest. Take my yoke upon you, and learn from me, for I am gentle and lowly in heart, and you will find rest for your souls. For my yoke is easy, and my burden is light." (Matthew 11:25-30)

Every commitment costs something, but, according to Jesus, this one costs much less than all the others. Consider this Lamb, Jesus–"Yeshua" (or "Yehoshuah"), "Yahweh is a saving cry"–Immanuel, "God-with-us," God as us, God among us, born in a barn, as helpless as any, with no place to rest his head, often homeless, hungry, thirsty, cold, and, in the end, humiliated and crucified. Slavery is not what it appears, and neither was this appearance of the Lamb. We could only expect that the infinite God of the universe would come as a picture of evolutionary perfection, armed to the hilt with tooth and claw and instinct and glory and power. But instead, he stood silent before the shearers. He gave his body as an offering and as food for many![196] He came in utter weakness to make known his utter competence as our Sovereign God, for which we will praise his name for an infinity of forevers! He came, as it were, with a marshmallow shooter to make his defeat appear plausible and

---

196 As Jesus said of himself, "the Son of Man came not to be served but to serve, and to give his life as a ransom for many." (Matthew 20:28)

to demonstrate that his "power is made perfect in weakness." (2 Corinthians 12:9)

You must close your eyes to the myth of a godless universe and you must open them to the reality. Out of the ground and in every place, with minimal effort, we find fuels that burn slowly and evenly for man to control and to keep himself warm. We cut down a tree to build ourselves a home and with the scraps we carve a bowl, start a fire, and the rest goes into the fire to cook the evening meal. Every back yard is a medicine cabinet and a veritable warehouse of delicacies, delights, and decadent designs, each of which prompts that interesting and inevitable question, *who designed this?* We plant a few seeds only to come back later to find "plants yielding seed, and fruit trees bearing fruit in which is their seed, each according to its kind,"[197] all of which are curiously delicious. We consume animals that seem *fittest* only for consumption–flat-toothed, slow, docile, defenseless, mushy things, which thrive on the grass that grows everywhere without any human exertion at all. And even the dumbest little creatures under the sun do the most profound deeds:

> Every spider is a versatile genius: It plans its web like an architect, and then carries out this plan like the proficient weaver it is. It is also a chemist who can synthesize silk employing a computer controlled manufacturing process, and then use the silk for spinning. The spider is so proficient that it seems to have completed courses in structural engineering, chemistry, architecture, and information science. But we know that this was not the case. So who instructed it? Where did it obtain this specialized knowledge? Who was its adviser? Most spiders are also active in recycling. They eat their web in the morning, then the material is chemically processed and re-used for a new web.[198]

---

197 Genesis 1:11
198 Gitt, *In the Beginning was Information*, 12.

We live in a world where information-code is hidden in everything, as so much software code, where unintelligent plants and cells act with purpose, and where days and distances and everything else can be neatly and conveniently counted and measured in simple, rational, *comfortable* intervals, as morning and evening and hour and season, to be numbered and quantified with mechanical and mathematical precision as awe-full, awe-some, awe-inspiring divine technology! The book of nature and the book of Scripture both speak plainly of the same God, and any view which ignores the data is bound to defeat itself in the long run. This God is the necessary inference of absolutely everything, the precondition of all design, all personality, all relationship, all love, all knowledge, and of everything; "self-consciousness presupposes God-consciousness."[199] "The fool hath said in his heart, There is no God."[200]

Have you not seen that in the sky there is a light that is the source of all life and warmth and radiance, apart from which we could neither see nor do anything at all? Much too glorious to look at without burning the eyes, it forces a natural choice between self-destruction or the bowed head of humility, and as the head is bowed toward this realm of shadows under the sun, our attention is directed to a shell of dust beneath our feet which conceals a core of lava that can only be described as a lake of fire.[201] In every corner we find things suitable to build shelter with, suitable to fashion technology, suitable to clothe ourselves with, suitable to eat and to drink, as if they *were suited to us*, not blandness unto survival, but luxury and affluence, every texture and taste and smell and sound and color attuned—as art—to the pleasure and satisfaction of man as the design of a master habitat-builder, as one who, like father to child, takes his satisfaction in our satisfaction, just as he wants us to turn back, to *re-pent*, and to once again find our satisfaction

---

199 Van Til, *The Defense of the Faith*, 90.
200 Psalm 14:1 ASV
201 Our sun is a sort of temporary stand-in for the true Son: "And the city [of heaven] has no need of sun or moon to shine on it, for the glory of God gives it light, and its lamp is the Lamb. By its light will the nations walk, and the kings of the earth will bring their glory into it, and its gates will never be shut by day—and there will be no night there. They will bring into it the glory and the honor of the nations. But nothing unclean will ever enter it, nor anyone who does what is detestable or false ..." (Revelation 21:23-26)

in him. Oh friend, you must close your eyes to the myth! And you must open your eyes to the reality that in the beginning, God created the heavens and the earth *for man,* and that his disposition—even now—is favorable unto you.

We must learn to look for the signs of deception and concealment. We must learn to account our lives a blessing rather than a punishment and a curse. We must learn to glory once again in our origin.

Afterword

For further reading about the Christian belief system, I commend to the reader the Holy Bible, 66 books written in 3 languages by about 40 different authors over approximately 1900 years–a story of slavery and redemption, an epic with an omniscient narrator–the consistent, trustworthy, historically-unfolding revelation of God, and, to an infinitely lesser degree, *The Westminster Confession of Faith*, John Calvin's *Institutes of the Christian Religion*, and Joel Beeke's *Reader's Guide to Reformed Literature*. All but the last are available online for free.

For further reading on presuppositionalism and presuppositional apologetics (the biblical-philosophical [abductive, indirect] method that I have adopted to a great extent in the present work), see Cornelius Van Til's *The Defense of the Faith* along with Greg Bahnsen's *Van Til's Apologetic: Readings and Analysis*.

For further reading in Christian philosophy, see Augustine's *Confessions*, Jonathan Edwards' *Freedom of the Will*, Van Til's *Introduction to Systematic Theology* and also Gordon Clark's *Thales to Dewey*, which is a very fine introduction to the history of philosophy from the Christian and Reformed perspective.

Semper Reformanda!

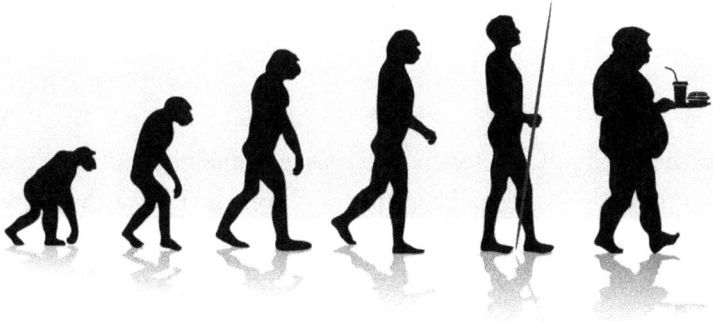

Evolution Evolves

T. Dougherty

The Book of Genesis, chapters 1-3

In the beginning, God created the heavens and the earth. The earth was without form and void, and darkness was over the face of the deep. And the Spirit of God was hovering over the face of the waters.

And God said, "Let there be light," and there was light. And God saw that the light was good. And God separated the light from the darkness. God called the light Day, and the darkness he called Night. And there was evening and there was morning, the first day.

And God said, "Let there be an expanse in the midst of the waters, and let it separate the waters from the waters." And God made the expanse and separated the waters that were under the expanse from the waters that were above the expanse. And it was so. And God called the expanse Heaven. And there was evening and there was morning, the second day.

And God said, "Let the waters under the heavens be gathered together into one place, and let the dry land appear." And it was so. God called the dry land Earth, and the waters that were gathered together he called Seas. And God saw that it was good.

And God said, "Let the earth sprout vegetation, plants yielding seed, and fruit trees bearing fruit in which is their seed, each according to its kind, on the earth." And it was so. The earth brought forth vegetation, plants yielding seed according to their own kinds, and trees bearing fruit in which is their seed, each according to its kind. And God saw that it was good. And there was evening and there was morning, the third day.

And God said, "Let there be lights in the expanse of the heavens to separate the day from the night. And let them be for signs and for seasons, and for days and years, and let them be lights in the expanse of the heavens to give light upon the earth." And it was so. And God made the two great lights—the greater light to rule the day and the lesser light to rule the night—and the stars. And God set them in the expanse of the heavens to give light on the earth, to rule over the day and over the night, and to separate the light from the darkness. And God saw that it was good. And there was evening and there was morning, the fourth day.

And God said, "Let the waters swarm with swarms of living creatures, and let birds fly above the earth across the expanse of the heavens." So God created the great sea creatures and every living creature that moves, with which the waters swarm, according to their kinds, and every winged bird according to its kind. And God saw that it was good. And God blessed them, saying, "Be fruitful and multiply and fill the waters in the seas, and let birds multiply on the earth." And there was evening and there was morning, the fifth day.

And God said, "Let the earth bring forth living creatures according to their kinds—livestock and creeping things and beasts of the earth according to their kinds." And it was so. And God made the beasts of the earth according to their kinds and the livestock according to their kinds, and everything that creeps on the ground according to its kind. And God saw that it was good.

Then God said, "Let us make man in our image, after our likeness. And let them have dominion over the fish of the sea and over the birds of the heavens and over the livestock and over all the earth and over every creeping thing that creeps on the earth."

> So God created man in his own image,
> in the image of God he created him;
> male and female he created them.

And God blessed them. And God said to them, "Be fruitful and multiply and fill the earth and subdue it, and have dominion over the fish of the sea and over the birds of the heavens and over every living thing that moves on the earth." And God said, "Behold, I have given you every plant yielding seed that is on the face of all the earth, and every tree with seed in its fruit. You shall have them for food. And to every beast of the earth and to every bird of the heavens and to everything that creeps on the earth, everything that has the breath of life, I have given every green plant for food." And it was so. And God saw everything that he had made, and behold, it was very good. And there was evening and there was morning, the sixth day.

Thus the heavens and the earth were finished, and all the host of them. And on the seventh day God finished his work that he had done, and he rested on the seventh day from all his work that he had done. So God blessed the seventh day and made it holy, because on it God rested from all his work that he had done in creation.

These are the generations of the heavens and the earth when they were created, in the day that the Lord God made the earth and the heavens.

When no bush of the field was yet in the land and no small plant of the field had yet sprung up—for the Lord God had not caused it to rain on the land, and there was no man to work the ground, and a mist was going up from the land and was watering the whole face of the ground— then the Lord God formed the man of dust from the ground and breathed into his nostrils the breath of life, and the man became a living creature. And the Lord God planted a garden in Eden, in the east, and there he put the man whom he had formed. And out of the ground the Lord God made to spring up every tree that is pleasant to the sight and good for food. The tree of life was in the midst of the garden, and the tree of the knowledge of good and evil.

A river flowed out of Eden to water the garden, and there it divided and became four rivers. The name of the first is the Pishon. It is the one that flowed around the whole land of Havilah, where there is gold. And the gold of that land is good; bdellium and onyx stone are there. The name of the second river is the Gihon. It is the one that flowed around the whole land of Cush. And the name of the third river is the Tigris, which flows east of Assyria. And the fourth river is the Euphrates.

The LORD God took the man and put him in the garden of Eden to work it and keep it. And the LORD God commanded the man, saying, "You may surely eat of every tree of the garden, but of the tree of the knowledge of good and evil you shall not eat, for in the day that you eat of it you shall surely die."

Then the LORD God said, "It is not good that the man should be alone; I will make him a helper fit for him." Now out of the ground the LORD God had formed every beast of the field and every bird of the heavens and brought them to the man to see what he would call them. And whatever the man called every living creature, that was its name. The man gave names to all livestock and to the birds of the heavens and to every beast of the field. But for Adam there was not found a helper fit for him. So the LORD God caused a deep sleep to fall upon the man, and while he slept took one of his ribs and closed up its place with flesh. And the rib that the LORD God had taken from the man he made into a woman and brought her to the man. Then the man said,

> "This at last is bone of my bones
> and flesh of my flesh;
> she shall be called Woman,
> because she was taken out of Man."

Therefore a man shall leave his father and his mother and hold fast to his wife, and they shall become one flesh. And the man and his wife were both naked and were not ashamed.

Now the serpent was more crafty than any other beast of the field that the LORD God had made.

He said to the woman, "Did God actually say, 'You shall not eat of any tree in the garden'?" And the woman said to the serpent, "We may eat of the fruit of the trees in the garden, but God said, 'You shall not eat of the fruit of the tree that is in the midst of the garden, neither shall you touch it, lest you die.'" But the serpent said to the woman, "You will not surely die. For God knows that when you eat of it your eyes will be opened, and you will be like God, knowing good and evil." So when the woman saw that the tree was good for food, and that it was a delight to the eyes, and that the tree was to be desired to make one wise, she took of its fruit and ate, and she also gave some to her husband who was with her, and he ate. Then the eyes of both were opened, and they knew that they were naked. And they sewed fig leaves together and made themselves loincloths.

And they heard the sound of the LORD God walking in the garden in the cool of the day, and the man and his wife hid themselves from the presence of the LORD God among the trees of the garden. But the LORD God called to the man and said to him, "Where are you?" And he said, "I heard the sound of you in the garden, and I was afraid, because I was naked, and I hid myself." He said, "Who told you that you were naked? Have you eaten of the tree of which I commanded you not to eat?" The man said, "The woman whom you gave to be with me, she gave me fruit of the tree, and I ate." Then the LORD God said to the woman, "What is this that you have done?" The woman said, "The serpent deceived me, and I ate."

The LORD God said to the serpent,

> "Because you have done this,
> cursed are you above all livestock
> and above all beasts of the field;
> on your belly you shall go,
> and dust you shall eat

all the days of your life.
I will put enmity between you and the woman,
and between your offspring and her offspring;
he shall bruise your head,
and you shall bruise his heel."

To the woman he said,

"I will surely multiply your pain in childbearing;
in pain you shall bring forth children.
Your desire shall be for your husband,
and he shall rule over you."

AND TO ADAM HE SAID,

"Because you have listened to the voice of your wife
and have eaten of the tree
of which I commanded you,
'You shall not eat of it,'
cursed is the ground because of you;
in pain you shall eat of it all the days of your life;
thorns and thistles it shall bring forth for you;
and you shall eat the plants of the field.
By the sweat of your face
you shall eat bread,
till you return to the ground,
for out of it you were taken;
for you are dust,
and to dust you shall return."

The man called his wife's name Eve, because she was the mother of all living. And the LORD God made for Adam and for his wife garments of skins and clothed them.

Then the LORD God said, "Behold, the man has become like one of us in knowing good and evil. Now, lest he reach out his hand and take also of the tree of life and eat, and live forever—" therefore the LORD God sent him out from the garden of Eden to work the ground from which he was taken. He drove out the man, and at the east of the garden of Eden he placed the cherubim and a flaming sword that turned every way to guard the way to the tree of life.

Authorities

A Beautiful Mind, Ron Howard, Universal Pictures, 2002.

Back to the Future, Robert Zemeckis, Universal Pictures, 1985.

Bartholomew, David. *God, Chance, and Purpose.* Cambridge, New York: Cambridge University Press. 2008.

Behe, Michael J. *Darwin's Black Box: The Biochemical Challenge to Evolution.* New York, New York: Free Press. 1996.

Boehm, Christopher. *Moral Origins.* New York, New York: Basic Books. 2012.

Brock, Stuart and Edwin Mares. *Realism and Anti-Realism.* Stocksfield, England: Acumen. 2007.

Burtt, E.A. *The Metaphysical Foundations of Modern Science.* Atlantic Highlands, New Jersey: Humanities Press. 1992.

Conee, Earl & Sider, Theodore. *Riddles of Existence: A Guided Tour of Metaphysics.* Oxford, New York: Oxford University Press. 2005.

Cook, Roy T. *Paradoxes.* Cambridge, UK: Polity Press. 2013.

Darwin, Charles. *Autobiography*. New York, New York: W.W. Norton & Company. 1993.

Darwin, Charles. *The Origin of Species by Means of Natural Selection*. Chicago, Illinois: Great Books of the Western World, Encyclopedia Britannica, Inc. 1993.

Darwin, Charles. *The Descent of Man and Selection in Relation to Sex*. Chicago, Illinois: Great Books of the Western World, Encyclopedia Britannica, Inc. 1993.

Dennett, Daniel C. *Darwin's Dangerous Idea*. New York, New York: Touchstone. 1996.

Dennett, Daniel C. *Freedom Evolves*. New York, New York: Penguin Books. 2003.

Dennett, Daniel C. *Elbow Room*. New York, New York: Penguin Books. 2004.

Dawkins, Richard. *Afterword* in *What is Your Dangerous Idea?* Edited by John Brockman. New York, New York: Harper Perennial. 2007.

Dawkins, Richard. *The Blind Watchmaker*. New York, New York: W.W. Norton & Company. 1996.

Dawkins, Richard. *The God Delusion*. New York, New York: Houghton Mifflin Company. 2008.

Di Blasi, Fulvio. *God and the Natural Law: A Rereading of Thomas Aquinas*. South Bend, Indiana: St. Augustine's Press. 2006.

Dougherty, T. *The Holy Trinity: A New Approach*. Ohio or thereabouts: self-published. 2008. (A second edition is forthcoming.)

Fight Club, David Fincher, 20th Century Fox, 1999.

Flew, Anthony. *A Dictionary of Philosophy*. New York, New York: St. Martin's Press. 1984.

Gitt, Werner. *In the Beginning was Information*. Bielefeld, Germany: Christliche Literatur. 1997.

Ghostbusters, Ivan Reitman, Columbia Pictures, 1984.

Guinness, Os. *Time for Truth*. Grand Rapids, Michigan: Baker Books. 2000.

Harris, Sam. *Free Will*. New York, New York: Free Press. 2012.

Harris, Sam. *The End of Faith*. New York, New York: W.W. Norton & Company. 2004.

Harris, Sam. *The Moral Landscape*. New York, New York: Free Press. 2010.

Hawking, Stephen and Leonard Mlodinow. *The Grand Design*. New York, New York: Bantam Books. 2010.

Hepp, Valentine. *Calvinism and the Philosophy of Nature*. Grand Rapids, Michigan: William B Eerdmans Publishing. 1930.

Hume, David. *An Enquiry Concerning Human Understanding*. Chicago, Illinois: Great Books of the Western World, Encyclopedia Britannica, Inc. 1993.

Kuhl, Steven. *The Nazi Connection*. New York, New York: Oxford University Press. 1994.

Kuhn, Thomas S. *The Structure of Scientific Revolutions*. Chicago, Illinois: University of Chicago Press. 1996.

Loux, Michael J and Dean Zimmerman, editors. *The Oxford Handbook of Metaphysics*. New York, New York: Oxford University Press. 2003.

Neitzsche, Friedrich. *Beyond Good and Evil*. Chicago, Illinois: Great Books of the Western World, Encyclopedia Britannica, Inc. 1993.

Oliphint, K. Scott. *Covenantal Apologetics*. Wheaton, Illinois: Crossway Books. 2013.

Pearcey, Nancy R & Thaxton, Charles B. *The Soul of Science: Christian Faith and Natural Philosophy*. Wheaton, Illinois: Crossway Books. 1994.

Pichot, Andre. *The Pure Society: From Darwin to Hitler*. Brooklyn, New York: Verso. 2001.

Piper, John. *Desiring God: Meditations of a Christian Hedonist*. Portland, Oregon: Multnomah. 1986.

Polkinghore, John C. *Science and Providence: God's Interaction With the World*. West Conshohocken, PA: Templeton Foundation Press. 2005.

Poythress, Vern S. *Philosophy, Science and The Sovereignty of God*. Phillipsburg, NJ: Presbyterian and Reformed. 1976.

Plantinga, Alvin. *God, Freedom and Evil*. Grand Rapids, Michigan: William B. Eerdmans Publishing. 1991.

Plantinga, Alvin. *Where the Conflict Really Lies: Science, Religion, & Naturalism.* New York, New York: Oxford University Press. 2011.

Prigogine, Ilya and Isabelle Stengers. *Order out of Chaos: Man's New Dialogue with Nature.* Boulder, Colorado: Shambhala Publications. 1984.

Ramm, Bernard. *The Christian View of Science and Scripture.* Grand Rapids, Michigan: William B. Eerdmans Publishing Company. 1978.

Rea, Michael C. *World Without Design: The Ontological Consequences of Naturalism.* Oxford: Oxford University Press. 2002.

Rocky, John G. Avildsen, United Artists, 1976.

Rushdoony, Rousas John. *The Mythology of Science.* Nutley, New Jersey: The Craig Press. 1968.

Schaeffer, Francis A. *How Should We Then Live?* Westchester, Illinois: Crossway Books. 1984.

Seinfeld, Larry David & Jerry Seinfeld, Castle Rock Entertainment, 1989-1998.

Shiang, David. *God Does Not Play Dice: The Fulfillment of Einstein's Quest for Law and Order in Nature.* Open Sesame. Kindle Edition.

Sproul, R.C. *Not a Chance.* Grand Rapids, Michigan: Baker Books. 1995.

The Big Lebowski, Joel Coen & Ethan Coen, Polygram, 1998.

The Matrix, Andy Wachowski & Lana Wachowski, Warner Brothers, 1999.

The Shawshank Redemption, Frank Darabont, Castle Rock Entertainment, 1994.

Van Til, Cornelius. *The Defense of the Faith*. Phillipsburg, New Jersey: Presbyterian and Reformed. 1967.

Walton, Douglas N. *Abductive Reasoning*. Tuscaloosa, Alabama: The University of Alabama Press. 2004.

Weikart, Richard. *From Darwin to Hitler*. New York, New York: Palgrave Macmillan. 2004.

Whitehead, A.N. *Science and the Modern World*. New York, New York: Free Press. 1967.

www.ingramcontent.com/pod-product-compliance
Lightning Source LLC
LaVergne TN
LVHW051416080426
835508LV00022B/3109